Understanding Ministerial Leadership

Essays contributing to a developing theology of ministry

John A. Esau, editor
Foreword by Ross T. Bender

Text Reader Series 6
1995

Institute of Mennonite Studies
Elkhart, Indiana

Text-Reader Series

Series Titles:

1. *Essays on Biblical Interpretation: Anabaptist-Mennonite Perspectives.* Edited by Willard M. Swartley, 1984.

2. *One Lord, One Church, One Hope, and One God: Mennonite Confessions of Faith in North America.* Howard John Loewen, 1985.

3. *Monotheism, Power and Justice: Collected Old Testament Essays.* Millard C. Lind, 1990.

4. *So Wide a Sea: Essays on Biblical and Systematic Theology.* Edited by Ben C. Ollenburger, 1991.

5. *Essays in Anabaptist Theology.* Edited by H. Wayne Pipkin, 1995.

The Text-Reader series is published by the Institute of Mennonite Studies with the encouragement of the Council of Mennonite Seminaries. The series seeks to make available significant resource materials for seminary classroom use. By using photographic reproduction and/or desktop publishing technology, and marketing primarily through individual channels, the series seeks to make available helpful materials at relatively low cost.

Priority in accepting manuscripts will be given to material that has promise for ongoing use in the seminary classroom, with orientation toward or interest in the Anabaptist-Mennonite theological tradition.

The Institute of Mennonite Studies is the research agency of the Associated Mennonite Biblical Seminary, 3003 Benham Ave., Elkhart, Indiana, 46517-1999.

Copyright © 1995 by the Institute of Mennonite Studies
ISBN 0-936273-22-4
Printed in the United States of America

Dedication

To the memory of Marlin E. Miller

who at the time of his death on November 3, 1994, was serving

as

President of Associated Mennonite Biblical Seminary

Elkhart, Indiana

In addition to the essay contributed to this volume, Marlin Miller was planning to write an additional essay during the three-month sabbatical which he was just beginning, dealing in more detail with the Pauline understandings of ministry and leadership in the church. Marlin was an able administrator, a theological scholar, and one who loved the church not only in its ideals but in the practical and often troubling realities of its institutional life.

Contents

List of Contributors

Duane Beck is pastor of the Belmont Mennonite Church in Elkhart, Indiana. He served as a writer and steering committee member of the Pastorate Project, a churchwide program to clarify and support congregations and pastors in their mutual relationships.

George R. Brunk III serves as the Vice President and Academic Dean of Eastern Mennonite Seminary of Harrisonburg, Virginia. As part of the teaching faculty there, he is Professor of New Testament.

John A. Esau serves as Director of Ministerial Leadership Services for the General Conference Mennonite Church. Prior to the current denominational position, he served twenty-two years in pastoral ministry, first as pastor of Faith Mennonite Church in Minneapolis, Minnesota, and then of the Bethel College Mennonite Church in North Newton, Kansas.

Ardean Goertzen served as pastor of the Oak Park Mennonite Church in Oak Park, Illinois. He was also one of the original writers for the Pastorate Project. Presently he is employed with the Social Services office of the State of Illinois.

Lydia Neufeld Harder served as an interim faculty member at Canadian Mennonite Bible College, Winnipeg, Manitoba, during the school year 1993-94. She resides in Toronto, Ontario, where she remains active in church and theological pursuits, presently as interim director of the Mennonite Theological Centre.

Marlin E. Miller was President of Associated Mennonite Biblical Seminary in Elkhart, Indiana, at the time of his untimely death in November 1994. Marlin had been involved in many theological and pastoral projects including serving as a member of the steering committee of the Pastorate Project and as a member of the writing team for the Mennonite Confession of Faith.

Renee Sauder is presently pastor of the Erb Street Mennonite Church of Waterloo, Ontario. Her earlier ministries were as Associate Pastor of Bethel College Mennonite Church, North Newton, Kansas, as chaplain at Bethel College, and as coordinator for Women in Ministry for the Mennonite Board of Congregational Ministries.

Rodney Sawatsky has served in teaching and administrative roles in several Mennonite institutions including Canadian Mennonite Bible College and Conrad Grebel College where he served as both academic Dean and as

President; currently he is President of Messiah College in Grantham, Pennsylvania.

Erick Sawatzky is Director of Field Education and Assistant Professor of Pastoral Ministry at the Associated Mennonite Biblical Seminary; Elkhart, Indiana. He has served as pastor of the Trinity Mennonite Church, Hillsboro, Kansas, and of Grace Mennonite Church, Regina, Saskatchewan; in addition, he has worked in prison chaplaincy ministry.

Marcus Smucker is Coordinator of Spiritual Formation and Associate Professor of Pastoral Theology at Associated Mennonite Biblical Seminary, Elkhart, Indiana. Prior to that he served as Pastor of the Portland Mennonite Church, Portland, Oregon.

Foreword

The essays in this collection are of more than casual interest to me for they bear directly on matters that have preoccupied me for the past four decades, namely, the meaning and practice of Christian ministry. Most of the essays begin on an autobiographical note so I will do the same. I was ordained to the Christian ministry in May 1958. I understood my ordination to be both a recognition by the church of my call to be a Christian minister and an acknowledgement on my part of my accountability to the church for the way I would carry out my ministry.

As a faculty member at Associated Mennonite Biblical Seminary (AMBS), both professor and dean, I became involved in discussions about the theology of ministry which underlies the curriculum of preparing persons for Christian ministry. There were vigorous debates in the Dean's Seminar in the latter part of the 1960s over the meaning and practice of pastoral ministry. The purpose of the Dean's Seminar was to develop a model for theological education in the Free Church tradition. The report of their work is found in Ross T. Bender, *The People of God* (Scottdale, PA: Herald Press, 1971).

A fundamental issue in contention was whether "Christian ministry" referred to that which was given by Christ to "the one or the many", that is, only to those who were ordained and set apart or also to the whole people of God. While there was recognition that there are two types of texts in the New Testament (the offices of the bishop, pastor, elder and deacon on the one hand and the gifts of the Spirit on the other), it is clear that the Dean's Seminar emphasized the latter texts.

During the second half of the 1980s I was called to be a pastor in Colorado and took an extended leave of absence from AMBS. These were fruitful years which enabled me, among other things, to look at the theology of Christian ministry from within the setting of the practice of pastoral ministry. The issues were no longer primarily theoretical but very personal and immediate. Although I had never doubted that pastoral ministry was vital to the health and wellbeing of the congregation and to the carrying out of its mission, I came to a new appreciation of that office as well as how important it is that there be clarity about how the pastoral role is shaped. I agree with Marcus Smucker (chapter IX) that "incarnational presence" is the defining essence of what pastoral ministry is and should be.

For several years I have been in conversation with John Esau about the development of this collection of essays and have looked forward to its publication in the Institute of Mennonite Studies Text Reader series. In his opening essay and in his selection of these particular papers and addresses, John is presenting a corrective to what he perceives to be an imbalance in the view of Christian ministry which emphasizes the ministry of the whole people of God at the expense of an adequate appreciation for the ministry of those who have been called out, set apart, trained and ordained. Sometimes this tension is stated in terms of gifts versus office. Since John identifies the work of the Dean's Seminar and the curriculum to which it gave rise as the position to be corrected, I think it appropriate to comment on them briefly.

But first let me say that I welcome John's initiative in this regard. He is in an excellent position to comment on the present situation in the churches with regard to the shape of the Christian ministry and the effects of several decades of seminary education according to the Theological Educational in the Free Church Tradition model. I welcome his insights gladly and I take seriously what he and the other writers have to say.

The heart of John's concern, as I understand it, is that the church recover an appreciation for the office of pastoral ministry. The emphasis on the ministries of the whole people of God of the past several decades, in his view, has tended to obscure and even to diminish the pastoral role and identity. A one-sided emphasis on the texts which speak of spiritual gifts (Romans 12, 1 Corinthians 12, Ephesians 4) has brought about a situation where pastors in particular are confused about their place in the church and even their very identity as pastors. Furthermore, the egalitarian and iconoclastic tendencies of the 1960s in relation to issues of leadership and authority in the church as well as in society have exacerbated this situation.

At the center of the issues being debated in the Dean's Seminar was the concern that all the functions of ministry should not be concentrated in one person, the seminary-trained, salaried professional pastor. The Seminar concluded that "the ministry which Christ gives to his followers is binding on all the members of his body" and that "this ministry is not just one's gainful employment in the secular realm but a job to be done in the corporate life of the congregation, in its worship, in its teaching, its preaching, its discernment of God's will, in its government, and in its diakonia in the world. " (Bender, 154)

These conclusions differ markedly from John's assertion in his opening essay that "in the case of the many, the people of God, the locus of their ministry is best understood as being primarily in the world; that is where they fulfill their vocation, their "*vocatio*" and that "in contrast the pastor's ministry is primarily focused within the church, for that is the locus of the pastor's vocation." (Esau, 6)

Although we disagree on this point, let me affirm some of John's convictions which I do share. First is that the office of pastoral ministry is an important one. It is identified in the New Testament along with several additional offices of Christian ministry. It is also identified in the Anabaptist and Mennonite traditions. John is correct in stating that this office belongs to the church and not to the individual minister. I agree with him that the office stands prior to the various functions that the pastor is called upon to perform. It is important to recognize the pastor's office, role and identity and not only the pastor's gifts, skills and functions.

The Pauline texts on the gifts of the Spirit do not, of course, exclude the gifts of leadership as though they are not among the gifts of the Spirit. Romans 12:8 makes reference to "he that takes the lead" or "the leader." Ephesians 4:11-12 specifically identifies several of the leadership gifts--apostles, prophets, evangelists, pastors and teachers--and states that their basic task is "to equip the saints for the work of ministry, for building up the body of Christ." These leadership gifts do not displace the gifts of the Spirit but are exercised in order to empower them.

In Romans 12:4 it is explicitly stated that "all the members do not have the same function," an explicit recognition that some pattern of organization and leadership is needed in order to avoid chaos and to promote health and good order. And the basic principle of organization is to be found in the body metaphor. It therefore becomes a matter of finding the most faithful and effective ways of organizing ministry in the church. The precise shape of ministry can and does change over the years, a development which is already evident in the New Testament texts themselves.

I am finding it helpful to recognize that a theology of Christian ministry is broader than a theology of pastoral ministry. Christian ministry includes pastoral ministry but is more comprehensive than that. It includes also the ministry of teachers and evangelists, for example. And it includes the ministries of the whole people of God. These should not be confused with each other as if they were the same thing, nor should they be pitted against each other. The ministry of the pastor and the ministry of the people belong together.

It seems to me important to hold these perspectives in tension, that there are indeed distinct leadership offices in the church and there are diverse gifts of the Spirit given severally by the Spirit as the Spirit chooses. Both teachings are to be found in the New Testament. Neither should be emphasized to the exclusion of the other. It is not a question of "the one or the many"; it is a matter of "the one and the many."

The present essays serve as a corrective to the emphasis of an earlier period when the pastoral ministry was not adequately recognized and appreciated. If, however, the next decades cause us to tilt in the direction of diminishing the ministries of the whole people of God, it is to be hoped that there will be those who bring a new corrective so that the ministry entrusted to the church by Christ, the head of the church, will be faithfully carried out.

Ross T. Bender, Director
Institute of Mennonite Studies
Elkhart, Indiana
February 1995

Preface

This project began in a conversation with Ralph Lebold in the halls of Associated Mennonite Biblical Seminary in Elkhart, Indiana. Over the course of several years, I had been in many different locations where significant presentations had been made related to emerging understandings of pastoral ministry. I knew that important things were being spoken which had not been heard for three decades in most Mennonite settings. New wineskins were containing new ways of understanding ministry.

The question Ralph and I talked about that day was: how do we preserve and make available to a broader audience these collected statements? What was typical was that these oral presentations were each being heard, received, affirmed, and then lost to public access. But if they were to help us to rethink our understandings of ministerial leadership in the church, we needed a format that would preserve and make them available for a sustained period of time and to a broader audience.

This collection of essays does not portend to present a complete and systematic treatment of the subject. That remains a project for another time and for a churchly scholar whose academic skills are matched by their love for and understanding of ministry. These are interim statements made with considerable passion by persons along the way.

Some of these statements come directly out of the experience of pastoral ministry. Some are by scholars speaking to pastors about the ministerial task. Still others come from within the more institutional confines of church bureaucracy. What unites these essays is an underlying assumption that the existing theology of ministry which has dominated the Mennonite church for at least a third of the twentieth century has not served us well.

This theology of ministry contained much idealism about notions of equality and egalitarianism within the church in which all members of Christ's body were called to ministry. It vigorously challenged notions of leadership which were authoritarian and hierarchical. It adopted a new set of words which spoke about ministers as "enablers, equippers, and servant leaders."

But what have been the results of that theology? For all of its idealism and apparent use of certain biblical images, we have been left with a theology that has failed. It spoke the language of "empowerment," but its prime effect has been the disempowerment of both pastor and congregation. It wanted to clarify the truth that everyone is a minister of God, but it resulted in a confusion of roles and conflicts that have had an undermining effect upon the church. Could it be that some of the congregational conflicts between pastors and their congregations are at least partially rooted in theological assumptions about leadership roles?

This egalitarian theology of ministry made claims to being both biblical and Anabaptist, which in Mennonite circles is the near equivalent of claiming papal infallibility. But time, second thoughts, and careful research have a way of undoing assumed truth. In reality, one could argue that these notions are more rooted in the cultural revolution that was part of what was happening in North America at the time of Vietnam and Watergate. It has been a time in which all those who have been perceived as professionals (doctors, lawyers, politicians, and pastors) have been challenged as to their role and legitimacy.

Though the essays that follow have only a limited basis in either biblical or historical studies, they do contain more than hints of emerging interpretations of both Scripture and Anabaptist history which suggest other alternative understandings and interpretations about leadership.

If I would give a label to the theology of ministry which is now being challenged in these essays, the words which I would be most likely to choose would be "a functionalist theology of ministry." It was assumed that if there was finally any justification for pastoral leadership, it was to fulfill certain tasks or functions needed by the church for which this or that person was best prepared and most capable of doing. It talked incessantly about what the church needed to have done and who had the "gifts" to perform those functions.

What this theology of ministry lacked was any understanding of the place of the pastoral "office." It explicitly rejected notions of representationalism, the concept that one person might symbolically speak and authentically act in behalf of the whole. Concepts about shared leadership tended to degenerate into meaning that the pastor lost the power and authority required to serve the church effectively. In its most crass form, pastors have spoken about having been "given the responsibility but not the authority" to lead, a position of obvious disempowerment.

While the essays which follow do address issues of scriptural interpretation and historical understanding, the element which binds them together is the experience-based reality of their perceptions. These are leaders of the church who are observing carefully not only the experience of others but also of themselves and the reality of their own ministry within the church.

They have learned not only from theory and theological formulations but also from the practice of ministry and their day-to-day life as persons who have offered the best of themselves to God's service.

It was out of the struggle to understand himself as a pastor that Marcus Smucker saw new biblical metaphors that enriched his understanding. It was in the experience of ministry that the women, whom Renee Sauder describes, learned to live with and grow beyond the dissonance between their inner call and their inner ambivalence. And, surprisingly, even Marlin Miller with his intellectual and scholarly proclivity chose to begin with his personal journey around ministry.

This collection of essays has an obvious bias; it makes no claim for balance or evenhanded debate. Its purpose is to restore balance to what has been lost. It seeks the restoration of understanding the office of ministry as that which God has given to the church for its health and well-being. It seeks the recovery of something rooted in the earlier tradition as true Anabaptists would, namely, that effective ministerial leadership is essential to effective mission that moves the church beyond self-serving preservation.

Having said that does not make one unaware of the dangers of constructing a theology of ministry too exclusively around the pastoral office. Reliance upon the ministerial office to compensate for the lack of personal and spiritual credibility is no gain; indeed, by itself it offers its own distortions and would defeat the goal of true servanthood leadership. As stated above, our goal is to restore balance, not to create a new imbalance.

In the larger scheme of things, we must move even beyond simple restoration; primitivism can be an evasion of a contemporary response and responsibility. Part of the theological task is always with a cast toward the future and the new images that can enhance and enlarge our vision. Hopefully, we can find within these essays insights that take us forward as a church. Re-imagining calls forth creative work, work that is shared with an ever-creating God who in the expanses of the universe must be busy about many things. In this sense, a viable theology of ministry will always be engaged in a missionary task.

Finally, I want to speak to the meaning of the phrase "theology of ministry." During the course of this project, Ralph Lebold put together a statement defining three closely related concepts; Lebold used the terms "practical theology," "pastoral theology," "and pastoral ministry."

As he interpreted these, practical theology is an academic discipline within the seminary or other educational institutions for the training of pastoral persons. As such, it stands alongside of biblical, historical, and theological disciplines. It has as its focus not only the training of scholars but specifically the formation of pastoral persons utilizing both theoretical- and experience-based learning. What separates practical theology from the other two is its rootedness in the seminary, the training institution.

In contrast is the term pastoral ministry which has to do with the practice of ministry within the context of the church. It has to do with occupation/vocation; and it is what one does in and for the church after having prepared oneself for that unique role of representational leadership. What separates pastoral ministry from the other two is its rootedness in the church and the practice of that vocational role.

Lebold's third term (although he lists it second) is pastoral theology. He defines it in this way: "Pastoral theology as a discipline constitutes theoretical reflections on ministry which provide guiding principles and a frame of reference governing the work of ministry." It has to do with how we think about ministry; it has to do with providing, interpreting, and critiquing conceptual models. This is the category which I prefer to speak of as our "theology of ministry."

In differentiation from the other two concepts but also in relationship to them, pastoral theology or the theology of ministry is a bridging term that is mutually related to both the seminary and to the church. It is ideally created out of the continuing dialogue between the seminary and its passion for clear and careful analysis and the church with its passion for wise and competent ministry. It is the bringing together into a conceptual whole the equally important disciplines of thought and praxis. It informs and forms our understanding of pastoral persons as to their being and their doing, as to their role and task, by means of creative theological reflection.

To the extent that this volume moves that dialogue of interpretation along for the benefit of the church and those who serve the church in the role of pastors and other forms of ministry in specialized settings, it will have served its intended purpose. That is, it will assist those who care about ministerial leadership to contribute further clarification to what is now a developing theology of ministry.

This collection of contemporary essays constitutes only one small contribution to the issues of a theology of ministry. Other projects that would merit attention and publication are the following: (1) Anabaptist historical statements that speak to the question, plus the ongoing interpretations of these materials. It might be important here to look for formal theological statements such as the confessions of faith, but equally important are other almost incidental statements that occur in historical documents that lend insight into earlier understandings. Liturgical sources would also make important contributions to our historical practice of ministry. (2) The twentieth-century institutional statements about ministry and ordination, both those whose origin was in the denominational and conference bodies of the church and those which originated from our seminaries and other institutions of ministerial education. (3) Biblical studies which speak to Mennonite interpretations of ministry and leadership within the church. (4) The most complete annotated bibliography of Anabaptist materials dealing with ministerial leadership was compiled by Bruce Hiebert while a senior at Associated Mennonite Biblical Seminary. The resources are rich for further research and interpretation. Several persons such as Gordon Zook, Earl Sears, and Keith Harder have already engaged in research and writing concerning ministry while completing the Doctor of Ministry degree.

Gratitude is always a Christian virtue, and certainly it is one of the key characteristics of those who lead the church with competence and grace. I too have learned how many persons contribute to what appears to be an individual process such as editing a volume of essays. At the front end of this project, three persons gave guidance in the form of a steering committee; they were Rodney Sawatsky, Anne Stuckey, and Ross T. Bender. As Director of the Institute of Mennonite Studies, Ross T. Bender stayed with the process with continuing words of encouragement to bring it to completion.

Perhaps most of all, I am indebted to the nine persons who made written contributions to this volume, all of whom did so with their only reward being the affirmation they might receive. Support and assistance came from my colleagues in the General Board office of the General Conference Mennonite Church, Vern Preheim and Shelley Buller. And finally, my thanks to my companion in life, in ministry, and in our common quest to understand leadership roles, my spouse, Bernice.

John A. Esau

December 31, 1994

Recovering, Rethinking, and Re-imagining: Issues in a Mennonite Theology for Christian Ministry

John A. Esau

The following essay was first presented to the faculty of Associated Mennonite Biblical Seminary, Elkhart, Indiana, on April 20, 1994.

I. Introduction: A Personal Journey into Ministry.

All theology contains within and behind it some form of autobiography. That is, our personal beliefs are deeply rooted in the stories of our life and faith; and these beliefs are in turn sorely tested as to their authenticity in the world of our experience. It is in the reciprocal encounter between these two realities that new understandings are given birth and then formed into new theological constructs.

My story does not begin with my ordination to ministry, but that is where I want to begin. I had recently graduated from Mennonite Biblical Seminary, which was itself a highly significant factor in the earliest formation of my theology of ministry. I was also coming to adulthood in the emerging world of what we eventually called "the sixties," with its passionate commitments to the ideologies of equality and egalitarianism. I was also young and idealistic (about twenty-six years old) with all the accompanying presumed certainties and real insecurities of a beginning pastor.

In reflecting back to that time, I have often recounted the fact that I felt no particular sense of call to pastoral ministry; neither had anyone in the church suggested as much to me. In the senior seminar at Mennonite Biblical Seminary a few years earlier, it was suggested to me (for reasons that I think I understand) that I ought to be thinking vocationally of something other than pastoral ministry. The fact that I became a pastor was more by default and job opportunity; I simply took what was there when I needed it. I recognize now that this is my human perspective on things; retrospectively, I can today also recognize divine providence in it all. The point is that I have no "call story" to tell other than a persistent awareness that my life would be lived out in some religious and specifically Christian vocational mode.

And now I was to be ordained. Memory has grown dim over the years, but such distant memories suggest that ordination also was almost a concession to convenience – so that I could legitimately carry out all the functions expected of a pastor. At the very least, I was determined not to be a "typical pastor," and certainly I did not want to assume any role or status that suggested ordination would place me spiritually above or separate from the congregation.

My father, Rev. J. J. Esau, known to many as the blind evangelist, was a part of every significant symbolic religious ritual in my life, and so, of course, I assumed his participation in my ordination. As the time approached, I shared with him my one request – that he not introduce me following the ordination ceremony as "Reverend."

His response was a question and it was also short and pointed: "But why are we doing this?" That moment was my introduction to the theology of ministry! Now I should add that as a gracious and understanding father, he did follow my request. And to this day I have avoided that title "Reverend," always preferring where titles are necessary something more related to the specific task.

However, what I have come to accept and to claim with considerable and surprising commitment is the mark that the ceremony of ordination placed upon my life, a mark that has had an enduring quality, almost an indelible quality in the defining of self. It was and remains a defining experience of identity which today I joyfully claim. More than I have claimed ministry as my vocation (calling – *vocatio*), ministry has claimed me.

It was in the lived experience of serving as a pastor that I found the inadequate theology of ministry with which I began to be sorely tested. What the congregation wanted and needed from me was more than the fulfilling of several tasks that needed to be done and for which they did not have the time nor the training. What they expected was someone who would accept a role, a role that would help to clarify their place and role within the church. What they needed was someone who in accepting that role of pastor would enable the congregation to function more effectively. What they intuitively looked for was a person who would symbolically embody the congregation in a representational manner.

Since that day of ordination in 1964, I have been on a thirty-year quest to better understand theologically what ministry is. I have long since concluded that the functionalist understandings with which I began ministry served not to strengthen but to undermine pastoral effectiveness. In its place

I have sought to discover a theology that would empower pastors to serve the church effectively, not for their personal aggrandizement but for the welfare and well-being of the church.

II. What Are the Sources for Theological Reflection and Therefore Sources of Authority?

It may seem strange to begin by asking a question dealing with theological method, but early on I ran into this question. I was in the office of a colleague several years ago when our conversation turned to the understanding of elders in the church. I don't remember much else, but I do recall vividly that chapter and verse were quoted to me in a way so as to signal the end of the conversation. I instinctively knew that I had been "proof texted," and I had the good sense not to argue. But I also knew that I was not satisfied with either this simplistic reduction of the question to whether or not I accepted the authority of the Bible, nor would I be satisfied with more sophisticated forms of biblical interpretation that might answer the ministry question differently.

What that experience signaled to me was that in all our theological reflection, which I understand to be a constructive human enterprise alongside of the divine revelation given for us to discern, we must make use of all the major components that shape our understanding. That is, we must find ways to use the Scriptures, to use the variety of Christian traditions that have informed the issues, particularly our own Anabaptist tradition, and to use our own contemporary lived experience within the ministry of the church as multiple sources to construct a viable theology of ministry.[1]

This reliance upon experience as a significant component for theological construction is the one that is most suspect, especially in light of

---

[1]George Brunk III preached a sermon at Bethel College Mennonite Church, North Newton, Kansas, on September 18, 1994, entitled "Discerning the Will of God." In it he raised the question whether the will of God was something that was disclosed or something to be discovered? The former places the activity of disclosure upon God; the latter places the task on the human activity of discovery. Brunk suggested a third option which he called discernment, thus combining disclosure and discovery. What happens when we begin to understand this as a dynamic collaboration in which we are called upon to think God's thought with God? This is another way of expressing the nature of a theological method which might prove helpful in understanding ministry.

the fact that it is so highly subjective and so dependent upon human experience, perception, and interpretation. Nevertheless, I want to argue that without it all our theology lacks authenticity and meaning; it also remains nothing more than an abstraction, however apparently rational or even biblical it may appear to be.

The recent movie *Shadowlands,* based upon the life of C. S. Lewis, is an extended narrative about the essential element of experience in the formation of theology. In the early part of the movie, C. S. Lewis is portrayed as the skillful lecturer on the meaning of suffering. But it is only after the experience of suffering through the death of his wife that Lewis comes to a more profound understanding – one no longer given to intellectual analysis but now given to the acceptance of the dreadful reality that can no longer be explained. It is then that Lewis says: "Experience is a harsh teacher. But you learn. My God, you learn."

Because of his experience of suffering, his theology about suffering was forever changed. No longer are we only given rational and intellectual analysis as to its meaning; what remains is the simple acknowledgment of the reality of suffering, the honest embracing of its pain, and the acceptance of something that is part of the human condition.

The question this raises is whether in using experience and tradition as a theological source we have not limited the unique authority of the Scripture. Have we then compromised the position of *sola scriptura* and ceased to use the Bible in a normative manner? My response is that practically speaking, that is precisely what everyone does, regardless of their theological orientation or even their lip service to the final authority of Scripture. But can we say more?

Particularly in the area of ministry and leadership, which was so clearly in a developmental stage within the first century, it is important to use the continuing experience of the church. The uniqueness (*sui generis*) of the Scripture needs strong affirmation as a primary source, forever an irreplaceable (*sine qua non*) and trustworthy source, to which we must always bring our traditions and our experience. Scripture is thus both a check on our subjective experience or our interpretations of the tradition; it is also an enduring source of new understandings. But it is not, it has never been, and can never be the only source for the church's task of theological construction.

The modality of theological reflection has been a creative source for contemporary theology, yielding more insightful and authentic understandings of faith in many areas of life and belief. What I am asking for is that now in our search for a more adequate and supportive theology of ministry, we turn again to our lived experience within ministry to gain more creative understandings growing out of our practice of ministry within the church.

III. The Ministry of the Many and the Ministry of the One?

One of the confusing issues over the last thirty years has been whether to define ministry as that which is given to the church as a whole and to each of its members, or whether ministry is to be understood in a more limited sense and related to leadership or even exclusively to the professional pastor. Common in that discussion has been the phrase "the priesthood of all believers," or as I have often heard it, "our Anabaptist concept of the priesthood of all believers." To invoke that phrase has been the Mennonite equivalent to invoking papal authority, and implicitly, to cast grave doubt as to whether we really do believe in pastoral ministry, with its attendant concerns for qualifications, education, credentials, and salaries.[2]

Marlin Miller has challenged this view in his article in Volume V of *The Mennonite Encyclopedia*, "Priesthood of All Believers."[3] Observing first of all that the basic concept was rooted in Luther's use of the phrase, Miller recalls Menno Simon's limited use of the phrase to call all believers to live holy and righteous lives. "And apparently neither Menno nor other Anabaptists and Mennonites of that time related the question of Christian ministry or the appointment and ordination of ministers in the church to the priesthood of all believers."[4]

Furthermore, the notion of the "priesthood of believers" is a common Christian theme, claimed again across the entire spectrum of Christian

---

[2]The primary document which articulated a theological rationale for this position came from a faculty seminar of Associated Mennonite Biblical Seminaries entitled *The People of God*, Ross T. Bender (Scottdale, Penn.: Herald Press, 1971). This document and particularly the chapter entitled "Theological Education in the Free Church Tradition" became the basis for the theological curriculum of the seminary and has cast its formation over a generation of Mennonite ministers and the church at large.

[3]The Mennonite Encyclopedia, Vol. V (Scottdale, Penn.: 1990), p. 721f.

[4]Ibid., p. 722.

theology; and we serve neither ourselves nor our Christian witness by thinking of it as a defining concept of Anabaptism. It is not.

To those conversant with the ecumenical literature dealing with the theology of ministry, you know that the concern as to whether ministry is for the Christian community as a whole or for those in designated leadership roles is a standard issue addressed across the spectrum of Christian traditions. And the answers are always the same: we believe and affirm that ministry in the church must always and consistently be defined by the both/and rather than by an either/or. Ministry is always both the ministry of the laity – the people – and the ministry of those called and ordained to a designated leadership role in which one person is symbolically representative of the whole.

There is another helpful way to differentiate between the ministry of the many, the people of God, and the ministry of the one, the pastor in the congregation. That is to define the primary locus of that ministry. In the case of the many, the people of God, the locus of their ministry is best understood as being primarily in the world; that is where they fulfill their vocation, their *vocatio*. This is not in any way to minimize their important role in the congregation in leadership and service; but it is to define their ministry at the center of their lives as finding fulfillment in the world that God still loves.[5]

In contrast, the pastor's ministry is primarily focused within the church, for that is the locus of the pastor's vocation. Again that is in no way to minimize the missionary character of pastoral ministry nor to deny the pastor access to ministry roles within the community and world. But it is to define more clearly the primary ministry of both the many and the one, given not from the edges and fringes of life but from its center, from its *vocatio*. This is the context in which we need to read and understand Ephesians 4:11f. "The gifts he gave were that some would be apostles, some prophets, some

---

[5]Precisely the opposite argument is made in *The People of God*. "For instance, we can say on the basis of New Testament authority that every member has a ministry (Romans 12:4-8; 1 Corinthians 12:4-31; Ephesians 4:4-16), that this ministry is not just his gainful employment in the secular realm but a job to be done in the corporate life of the congregation, in its worship, in its teaching, its preaching, its discernment of God's will, in its government, and in its *diakonia* in the world, p. 154. My argument with this is not whether members are involved in the life and leadership of the congregation, which they certainly are; the debate is around primary and vocational involvement in the church which is most often normative for the pastor in a way which is not true for other members.

evangelists, some pastors and teachers, to equip the saints for the work of ministry, for building up the body of Christ. . . ."[6]

The interpretation of these two verses has significantly shaped two contrasting visions about the nature and role of leadership within the church. The traditional interpretation is given in *The Interpreter's Bible*, both in the Exegesis and in the Exposition.[7] In seeing this passage as confirming the vital and essential place for a set-apart ministerial leadership for the church, Beare comments: "As God gave Christ to the church to be its head, so Christ has given ministers to the church to serve it in various functions."[8]

In contrast is the commentary by Markus Barth, who entitles this section of Ephesians as "The church without laymen and priests."[9] Barth summarizes his interpretation thus: "Are, therefore, the existence and function of a clergy simply dispensable? Indeed, the traditional distinction between clergy and laity does not belong in the church. Rather, the whole church, the community of all the saints together, is the clergy appointed by God for a ministry to and for the world."[10]

---

[6]Some have interpreted this passage as defining a fivefold ministry for the church. It is my view that this is simply an example of a stylistic feature of Pauline writing using a listing technique to cover a variety of examples of types of ministry present in the church within the first century. It was not intended nor has it traditionally been understood as a prescriptive list for forms of ministry within the church in all times and places. Rather, what we have here are expressions of what today are often referred to as "ministry in specialized settings."

[7]*The Interpreter's Bible, Vol. X*; Exegesis by Francis W. Beare, Exposition by Theodore O. Wedel. Is there any irony or significance that Theodore Wedel grew up in a General Conference Mennonite context as the son of the first President of Bethel College and became the Canon of the Washington Cathedral (Episcopal)! Wedel comments in his Exposition: "Divisiveness in Christendom has been symbolized by nothing so clearly as by differences in the theory of the ministry." (Abingdon Press, New York, 1953), p. 690.

[8]Ibid., p. 690.

[9]*The Anchor Bible: Ephesians*, Vol. 34A. Markus Barth (Doubleday: Garden City, New York, 1960), pp. 477-484.

[10]Ibid., p. 479.

However, Barth must be given credit for a more nuanced and better balanced interpretation than the above might lead one to believe. He cannot ignore the fact that this passage does speak about leadership roles in the church, all of which in some way share in "the ministry of the word."

However, the ministry of which Paul speaks in verse 12 is just as well translated by the word "service"; it is derived from *diakonia*, a verbal form of the noun for deacon. If one interprets this passage as calling all members of the Christian community to ministry, what is one to do with the fivefold gifts, each of which seem to have a unique role within the church? Is it not this group's task to prepare the entire congregation for service?

We are not told where this service is to occur. Is it within the community? Or is it more likely to be their service in their everyday life in the world? Both are conceivable and indeed necessary. But even what they have to offer within the church does not displace the validity or essential and unique role of the gifted leaders.

The immediate context is speaking to the unity of the church and to Christian maturity in a setting where division and conflict were more evident. The ultimate purpose of the gifts for leadership persons is to bring the church to the "unity of faith." This defines the pastoral task.

Another way to read the fivefold ministry gifts is to see them in the contemporary terms of "ministry in specialized settings." Not everything of either ministry or service occurs within the confines of the congregation. There is always a missionary task in the world to which the church is called, both as evangelists and the whole people of God.

The priesthood of believers has meaning because priesthood (ministerial leadership) has meaning and clarity and definition. If priesthood has no meaning or significance, the priesthood of believers is emptied of its powerful image for the ministry of God's people with its focus and its locus in the world.

IV. The Pastoral Self: Who Has the Gifts for Ministry?

One of the most common themes in settings where prospective new pastors are being nurtured is the discussion of whether or not one has the gifts for ministry. What is reflected in that exchange is an awareness that not everyone is capable of the leadership role that ministry apparently demands. It further reflects, usually implicitly, that not all of us are sufficiently teachable so as to gain the necessary gifts by means of education. The gifts for ministry and the pursuit of theological education are two very different things.

The language of "gifts" is so clearly drawn from the New Testament in passages such as Romans 12:3-8; 1 Corinthians 12; and Ephesians 4:7-16. In each of these passages there is reference to ministry roles within the church. And, of course, the implication is always that some persons have been given the special gifts for that purpose; that is, they have the abilities required to do certain things – ministry things – that constitute a role or at least a task within the faith community.

So the question appears to be important: do I, do you have the gifts for ministry? In the typical response, we have looked for answers to that question along the lines of the following: Do I have some skills for public speaking? Do I have an aptitude for theological issues or even the study of the Bible? Do I have charisma?

Each of those things properly interpreted is important to any and every pastor's potential success in ministry. But for the sake of argument here, I would suggest that these are neither the gifts for ministry nor the understanding of the gifts within the biblical passages. The Pauline concept of gifts reflects his attempt to find positive ways to interpret what otherwise is a problem of diversity and division within the church. Seeing in diversity the grace-filled gifts to the church is Paul's way to forge a unifying answer to what is otherwise a problem of members in competition and conflict over their personal priorities for the church.

Most of the time our primary fascination with ministry gifts points us in the direction of what some persons are able to do. And ministry does call for action and therefore for skills to be learned and competently performed. But they are not the primary gifts that any of us bring to ministry.

What is needed is to refocus the issue of gifts away from what we can do to who we are. The real issue is not in our doing but in our being. It is the quality of character that is the real issue, because the primary gift anyone brings to ministry is not their talents but their self. It is this internal person that we have come to know as "the self" in today's psychological orientation or in the biblical language where it is referred to as the heart and the soul.

Who we are and the capacity to make our lives a meaningful resource to the church and its members is our gift. That helps to understand why persons with significant injuries to the self that have not been healed are so routinely dysfunctional in ministerial leadership roles. They may be able to do what appears to be all the right things, but the real gift of a self redeemed by God's grace is not there and hence is not available to others. Karen Lebacqz in her book dealing with ministry, *Professional Ethics: Power and Paradox*, summarizes this when she writes: "A professional is called not simply to do something but to be something."[11]

One finds an insightful list of qualifications for ministry in the Pastoral Epistles where the author identifies qualities of character rather than gifts for those who would lead the church in bishop and deacon roles.[12] Here the tests of character measure the relationships of the self to the capacity of the person for effective ministry both in the church and in the world.

Understanding the self is a marvelously complex and wonderful subject that we must pursue in our search for quality ministry. Here more than anywhere else, psychology and theology intersect in ways that can enrich both disciplines. I have been particularly intrigued by the insights of Heinz Kohut in his theories of the self as formed by mirroring, merging, and alter ego.[13] In layperson's (here meaning those of us who are not professional psychologists) language, the self is formed by affirmation, by identification with and commitment to that which is perceived as greater than oneself, and by experiencing mutually shared relationships or community with those who are one's peers. Does this forming of the self have anything to do with theological education in the shaping of the person as a gift to the church through ministry? I believe it does.

To summarize this section, one of the key components that any of us bring to our roles of ministerial leadership within the church is the person we are, complex and wonderful, often with elements of mystery and creativity, always, of course, fully human and imperfect but nevertheless as a "treasure in clay jars," as Paul so accurately spoke in his powerful metaphor in 2 Corinthians 4:7.

---

[11]Karen Lebacqz, *Professional Ethics: Power and Paradox* (Nashville: Abingdon Press), p. 71. This is an important book for helping us to understand the unique roles and responsibilities of what it means to be a professional minister, holding an office in and on behalf of the church.

[12]See especially 1 Timothy 3:1-13.

[13]Robert Randall, *Pastor and Parish: The Psychological Core of Ecclesiastical Conflict* (New York, Human Sciences Press, Inc.). In this volume, Randall uses the basic concepts drawn from Heinz Kohut and his theories of the formation of the self.

V. Can Anabaptists Speak about the Office of Ministry and What It Means?

It was our last afternoon in Anchorage, the end of a very special vacation that my wife, Bernice, and I had shared in an Alaskan journey. I had spotted a Catholic church and bookstore across the street from our hotel; with the usual attraction to a bookstore, I went in to browse. Shortly I came across a book by the title *The Meaning of Christian Priesthood*[14] by Gisbert Greshake. Having already started on this project dealing with the theology of ministry, I pulled the book off the shelf to see if anything interesting might come from Catholic sources. Turning to the table of contents, I read: "The theological significance of church office as representation of Christ" and "A trinitarian concept of ministry." Here were the very concepts that had been shaping my thinking in recent months. I bought the book.

As I began to read, I quickly discovered that what Greshake was about was to develop a corrective to the theology of ministry that had emerged from post-Vatican II. What he saw in Catholic theology was the swinging of the pendulum from its earlier highly authoritarian and hierarchical stance to an understanding of ministry based upon notions of equality. Ministry was no longer rooted in Christ but in the church. As he perceived it, recent Catholic theology of ministry had brought about a great leveling and a functionalist approach to ministry that Greshake perceived as dysfunctional. His goal was not to restore the earlier distortions of authoritarianism, but to bring balance and a corrective to the debates of "the sixties."

What amazed me was the realization that the great theological shift in understanding ministry which we had defined as "Anabaptist recovery" was in fact more rooted in the political, cultural, and sociological realities of the modern era. The debates were the same; even the language was the same. And here was a Roman Catholic attempting to do precisely for them what I considered to be an urgent agenda for Mennonite ministry, namely, the reconstruction of a theology of the ministerial office in a way that maintained balance, or to use an emerging formula, polarity management.[15] I told my wife that it was worth the trip to Alaska just to gain that insight and understanding!

---

[14]Grisbert Greshake, *The Meaning of Christian Priesthood* (Dublin, Four Courts Press Ltd., 1982, Translation, 1988).

[15]Barry Johnson, *Polarity Management: Identifying and Managing Unsolvable Problems* (Amerst: HRD Press, Inc., 1992).

A. Office in Anabaptist History.

So what is the Anabaptist story in regard to our understanding of ministry? As indicated earlier, we had allowed the theological slogan of "our Anabaptist concept of the priesthood of all believers" to become the determining formula for our theology of ministry. What this has popularly come to mean is that we are disposed to think that if we were truly Anabaptist, we would not have professional clergy, since all Christians are priests to each other and all are ministers of Christ. More recent slogans such as "baptism is the ordination of the laity" have added strength to the convictions of some that we ought to be anticlerical Christians. That we are not is perceived as our compromise and accommodation to the so-called "Protestant model."

It is ironic to note that the defining concepts in these slogans are drawn from the set-apart ministry tradition. Priesthood and ordination have meaning because they are rooted in a lived and experienced reality; but if that reality is denied, why are they given theological power? As metaphors to define the heightened sense of all God's people and the place of each of us in the church, they carry great meaning. It is absurd, however, to use these as defining concepts to negate the very role upon which they are based.

John Howard Yoder, who more than anyone has helped to shape the recent theology of ministry within the church, at least is aware and ready to acknowledge that his anticlerical stance is not rooted in sixteenth-century Anabaptism. Indeed, he calls it "the unfinished reformation" precisely because he knows that the Anabaptist reformers "should not be looked to for special guidance or illumination on the matters of how to renew ministerial patterns, . . ."[16] Indeed, he adds later, "The universalism of ministry is the radical reformation that is still waiting to happen.[17]

Now it is true that the sixteenth-century Anabaptists offered a severe critique of the nonreformed clergy; Menno Simons, in particular, is vigorous in his denunciations.[18] But if one looks carefully at that critique, it seems to

---

[16]John Howard Yoder, *The Fullness of Christ* (Elgin, Ill.: Brethren Press, 1987), p. 41.

[17]*Servants of the Word: Ministry in the Believers' Churches,* David B. Eller, ed. (Elgin, Ill.: Brethren Press, 1990), p. 53.

[18]*The Complete Writings of Menno Simons* (Scottdale, Penn.: Herald Press, 1956), pp. 207f., 299f., 508f.

me that what we see there is the very legitimate rejection of those who claim the ministerial office but whose life and person does not correspond to the claims of the gospel. It is not the ministerial office which is rejected; rather, it is the abuse of that office by persons who have never earned the personal credibility within the church to serve within what Menno called "the high and holy office" of ministry.[19]

It is significant that all the major Anabaptist confessions when speaking about ministry and leadership in the church speak of the "office" of ministry as evidenced in the following excerpts, taken from over the last five centuries of Mennonite history.[20]

> Schleitheim 1527 – "The office of such a person (Shepherds in the congregation) shall be to read and exhort and teach."

> Dordrecht 1632 – "Regarding the offices and elections of persons . . . the church cannot exist or prosper . . . without offices and regulations."

> Ris Confession 1766 – "Christ . . . instituted various offices and conditions in his church."

> Mennonite Articles of Faith 1836 – Elbing, Germany (Eblag, Poland). "We believe that the ministry in the church is a divine institution." (Here the term office is not used, but "divine institution" is certainly its equivalent.)

> Articles 1933 (never officially accepted) – "God has appointed the office of ministry in its diversified duties and departments."

The point is that by both formal confession and by clear practice the Mennonite church and those within the Anabaptist faith tradition have carried a concept of the ministerial office in which persons were called by God and by the church to exercise a ministerial leadership role within and on behalf of the congregation of God's people.

---

[19]*The Complete Writings of Menno Simons*, John Christian Wenger, ed. (Scottdale, Penn.: Herald Press, 1956), p. 162. "For no one can serve in this high and holy office conformable to God's will, except he whom the Lord of the vineyard has made capable by the Spirit of His grace."

[20]*The Anabaptist Confessions*, Howard Loewen, ed. (Elkhart, Ind.: Institute of Mennonite Studies, 1985). The following excerpts are all to be found in this volume.

At times within our history the ministerial office has been abused, particularly by forms of authoritarian rule of the church when leadership has accumulated to itself power and authority that were no longer accountable to the whole body. It is unfortunate, however, that we have felt it necessary to negate a valued tradition as our response to the inappropriate use of power. What has happened approximates the image of Jesus that in casting out one demon, seven others have been allowed to enter.[21]

B. To Whom Does the Ministerial Office Belong?

In part, these abuses of power are perhaps the result of a misunderstanding as to whom the ministerial office belongs. There is a persistent notion that this office belongs to the person in ministerial leadership. That is a grievous theological error and one which needs our strongest challenge. The office of ministry belongs to the church, not to the person to whom the church has entrusted it.

As ministers, we have been given this ministerial office to occupy it in a representational role in behalf of the church, as long as we do so in ways that the larger church can affirm and which we by faithful service to the church can properly earn. We are stewards of the office. But it is not our office; it is the church's office of ministry. And the church has the right, indeed the responsibility, to remove us from that office when it is abused.[22]

In an age when we are coming to greater clarity about the necessity of accountability within leadership roles,[23] it is essential to understand that the ministerial office is precisely the locus within the church's accountability systems where there is leverage for discipline. Our recent involvement in

---

[21]Matthew 12:45.

[22]In somewhat typical fashion, what the church has done in responding to the abuses of persons by their authoritarian style, we have sought to remedy the problem by the changing of the structures (eliminating the office of bishop/aeltestor), rather than by challenging the abuse of power. The effect has been to create a vacuum of appropriate power which long tradition and experience has demonstrated as necessary.

[23]A recent attempt to restate the importance of ministerial accountability is a paper by Keith Harder, Support and Accountability of Pastors in the Western District Conference of the General Conference Mennonite Church (unpublished document submitted to the St. Paul School of Theology as his "Praxis Credo" in candidacy for the degree of Doctor of Ministry, 1994).

issues of sexual abuse has demonstrated how important the office of ministry is in the giving and withdrawing of credentials.

Intrinsic to the office of ministry is the representational element. While pastors offer themselves as a gift to the church, what they give is always more than themselves. What they represent is both the church and the One who is the Lord of the church. In other words, they fill a powerful symbolic role as they minister to and with the congregation of God's people in which "the whole is always greater than the sum of its parts." How strongly can we say this without moving into heresy? (Isn't heresy almost always the distortion of those truths which has crossed the threshold of believe-ability?)

Ministers represent God; at least that's the assumption of many. And if you can't claim that (and most ministers have trouble with this one), at least we must say that ministers portend to represent that which calls people to spiritual and transcendent reality.

Ultimately, thus ministry is derived from the messianic ministry of Jesus the Christ. The ministerial office most truly belongs to him. But in giving to Peter the keys of the kingdom, Christ symbolically gave this representational role to the church.[24] Certainly Anabaptists do not look to this passage for any legitimation of apostolic succession within the ministerial office, but to understand that ministry is rooted in Christ and the church rather than within an individual.

Having claimed that the ministerial office within the church is derived from the ministry of Jesus and constitutes his gift to the church, we should go on to ask how this ministry is formed and comes to life as we seek to find in Jesus' ministry our own ministry. There would be a very fruitful and important agenda for theological education to pursue this, even to the very practical questions of curriculum and educational methodology.

C. The Empowering Nature of the Office for Effective Ministry.

Among the several misperceptions that exist around the concept of a ministerial office, none is more prevalent than the notion that the purpose is to grant to the minister a position of prestige and personal power. This position of honor is understood popularly as something for the benefit of the minister, and thus it is naturally viewed with suspicion and often responded to by rejection of the minister him/herself.

---

[24]Matthew 16:18, 19.

In an egalitarian age such as our own where we have seen a great leveling of society and the loss by all professions of any automatic authority or even credibility, this sensitivity to and critique of an elitist notion within the church is well understood and should be applauded. The church does not need and God does not want those who are "servants" to be elevated in position above others. Those holding the ministerial office within the church are only of equal value to God and to God's kingdom as all others.

Once again we must return to asking about the true nature of the ministerial office and what it offers to God's servants to empower them for ministry. As long as we depend solely upon the gifts and talents which persons bring to ministry, we depend upon that which is fleeting and fallible. What the office of ministry does is to lend increased strength and unique empowerment beyond ourselves to fulfill our ministry for Christ and the church.

I recently was asked how it is that any young pastor has any significant role in ministering to those older than him/herself? The implied notion is that life experience only empowers one to minister to one's equal in age or younger. In effect, it's the same question about how a single pastor can do marriage counseling. As long as ministry depends solely upon the person and their experience, such limitations might be understood. But what is not understood in these questions is the empowering nature of the office that both enables and demands that we serve in a representational role that transcends what age we are or what we have experienced of life.

Most people have at some time experienced the added strength of an office to carry out tasks that they are expected to perform, knowing that they did this not only because of their giftedness but because others carried expectations and role perceptions of them. When we function within clearly defined roles to which others have called us, we know ourselves to be empowered and strengthened by the community that we serve.

Public leadership always places persons in highly vulnerable situations. Pastoral leadership is especially so, being the highly political position we have made it, in which to serve effectively one must have the support and confidence of the overwhelming majority of persons being served. The ministerial office offers at least a small degree of protection. But more than that, it intends to offer to those who occupy that office in the church's behalf several identifiable rights and privileges that will empower them to serve more effectively.

Among other things, the following might be identified: (1) An established position from which to speak to and for the church in a way that is not granted to everyone. (2) The right to enter without specific invitation into personal and family situations calling for pastoral care. (3) Access to information and other forms of power. (4) Access to groups and decision-making bodies in the church with whom leadership is shared. (5) The opportunity to offer vision for the future and to give leadership to help the church achieve that vision.

By accepting the privilege of being a steward of the church's ministerial office, we accept certain responsibilities and reasonable expectations that are placed upon us. Among these are the following: (1) An obligation to proclaim, interpret, and defend the Christian gospel. (2) A commitment to love and care for the church, even when one is compelled to be prophetically critical of it. (3) A duty to represent the church when its symbolic presence is needed, particularly in pastoral care. Also included in this symbolic representation may be those occasions calling for a prophetic voice and presence. (4) An obligation to live and act ethically and without partiality in all relationships. (5) A willingness to fulfill the tasks expected by the church to the best of one's abilities to do so. (6) A readiness as the servant of Christ and the church to act sacrificially and without need for acclaim when duty demands it.

Finally, the office of ministry calls for the person who occupies it to submit to both supervision and accountability. This will include at least the following areas: (1) For one's formal ministerial credentials. (2) For the servanthood manner in which one works and serves within the church, including one's stewardship of time. (3) For continuing growth as a person and as a pastor. (4) For living an example of high moral standards consistent with the new life to which all Christians are called. (5) For the exercise of stewardship of body, mind, and spirit as well as good stewardship of possessions, of financial resources, and of the earth.

D. Four Components of Representational Significance in the Office of Ministry.

A Scripture text that continues to powerfully form my Christian vision as well as to shape the parameters of my understanding of ministry is our Lord's summary statement of the Law: "Hear, O Israel: the Lord our God, the Lord is one; you shall love the Lord your God with all your heart, and with all your soul, and with all your mind, and with all your strength"

(Mark 12:29-30).[25] These four components have at least symbolic value for pointing toward four ways in which the Christian minister is called upon to serve in a representational role. Ministry must be lived out of the full person that we are: emotional, spiritual, intellectual, and physical.

1. Emotional: Those who would serve the church in a representational form are called upon to love and care for the church. It takes on an almost parental-like quality that offers wisdom and love to the community. Here it is essential to emphasize that this love is not just that given to individuals within the church, but to the church in its very institutional form. There is a sustaining quality to this love that transcends the foibles and failures of this all-too-human institution, thus communicating the minister's identity with the faith community.

2. Spiritual: What is the spiritual representational responsibility of the minister and how are we to understand and accept it? Is there a priestly dimension to Mennonite ministry that we can and must authentically claim? In an age in which spirituality has taken on an almost consumer mentality for the betterment of the self, might it be possible to reclaim a pastoral spirituality that is lived for the sake of the church and which offers itself as an empowering form of ministry? Might the pastor in this representational form be understood as the icon pointing beyond ourselves to the transcendent God? Could we thus claim to embody, however tentatively and imperfectly, the presence of God through the mystery of grace?[26]

3. Intellectual. Here I would understand the pastoral role as a leader in a representational way. The responsibility of such a person is to think and see clearly, offering vision and giving direction to the community.[27] As

---

[25]A careful exegesis of this passage would have to deal with questions relating this text with its Old Testament origins in Deuteronomy 6:4f and the comparable texts in Matthew and Luke. One must be careful not to ascribe modern psychological understandings of the human person to these texts, all of which have as their purpose to describe the total and complete response of humans to God.

[26]2 Corinthians 3:18.

[27]A proper understanding of vision is important here. A very helpful and at the same time delightful article was recently written by Craig Dykstra of Lilly Endowment, Inc. He suggests that vision is not so much "compellingly attractive views of the future that stir wonderment" but the ability to perceive clearly and accurately the present reality. *Initiatives in Religion*, Winter, 1994; Vol.3, No. 1.

leader, the pastor exercises that leadership through administrative and organizing skills. Another key intellectual component is the minister as the theologian-in-residence in the congregation. Here the pastor offers to the church the missionary role as the interpreter and defender of the faith. In this role the minister lives out a true intellectual love for God.

4. Physical. The very physical presence of the pastoral person as the living symbol of the church is perceived as the church's representative, whether in the pulpit or in the community. In this representational form, the church looks to the pastor to embody something of their collective self, their hopes, their dreams, their reality.

VI. Uniting the Person of the Minister and the Office of Ministry for Effective Functioning in the Tasks to Which We are Called.

Ultimately, every person in ministry in and for the church is expected to carry out some particular tasks. This is true whether the person has been called out of a lay ministry tradition without formal education or salary as well as those who are called to ministry in the church as educated through seminary degrees and serving as salaried professionals. In either case, the call today is to serve well with high degrees of competence and authenticity.

However, it has historically been difficult for the church and for ministers within the church to maintain the proper balance between the person we are and the office we hold. We have not always understood the reciprocal nature of these two key components and how essential one is to the other for effective functioning in the ministerial tasks.

It is always easy for persons in leadership roles to slide into an undue dependence upon the office they have been given, assuming that office alone holds sufficient power to carry the authority so necessary to ministry. Inevitably, that slide into reliance upon the ministerial office has led to authoritarianism and assorted forms of legalism. When that happens, authenticity is soon lost, relationships no longer matter, and effective ministry disappears.

On the other hand, when the church has needed to offer a corrective to move away from the bondage of ministerial reliance upon the office, the tendency has been to swing across the pendulum to where there is a denial of the office and an attempt to establish ministry solely upon the person and the assorted gifts that reside within the person. One of the downsides of this swing of the pendulum has been the cult of personality, in which the church thrives only as long as the gifted leader is present. In its most simple form, this functionalist theology has asked what it is that is needed within the church and then asked who had the gift to meet that need. Let them be called to minister for a time.

The urgent need today is to restore the balance and to reclaim both person and office as essential to each other for effective ministry.[28] We must forge a new synthesis, to use Hegelian language. Or to use more contemporary images from modern management theory, we must regain an understanding of "polarity management," which is able to live with the values inherent in opposing polarities and gain the benefits of both.[29]

In this model, office and person represent two poles of authority. Each of them has positive aspects and outcomes based upon their effectiveness, but they may also have potential negative consequences that must be taken into account. It is possible to rely on one or the other, but when one does, the likelihood is that over time the positive outcomes will diminish and the negative consequences will prevail. The trick is to claim both office and person and to thrive off of the positive benefits that each have to offer when they are in balance and mutually contributing to effective ministry.[30]

Within the person we are, we gain access to the church's call to fulfill its office of ministry. But having been given the office, one must continue to daily earn the right to occupy that office in behalf of the church. It is living

---

[28]Jackson W. Carroll, in his book *As One with Authority* (Louisville: Westminster/John Knox Press, 1991), argues for the same balance: "...authority of office and personal authority are mutually reinforcing," p. 57. Carroll describes the expertise of the office as certified competence and the expertise of the person as demonstrated competence.

[29]Barry Johnson, *Polarity Management: Identifying and Managing Unsolvable Problems* (Amherst: HRD Press, Inc., 1992).

[30]Ministry embodies a multitude of polarities which must be managed for effective leadership in the church. Without pretending to be exhaustive, I have identified thirty such combinations which if managed well can contribute to both survival and success in ministry. Examples might be such combinations as: planning long term – planning short term; being a teacher – being a learner; being a person of prayer – being a person of action, etc.

with a lifetime of reciprocity between these two polarities that one grows in ministry and gains the confidence of the church.[31]

The minister lives forever in the midst of a paradox that cannot and must not be resolved. As one fully human, equal in all respects to all members within the body of Christ, dependent upon the grace and forgiveness of God and sharing as one among all others the inheritance of faith, the minister stands within the church as a "joint heir" of the fullness of life in Christ. But as one called by God and the church in this representational role, the minister is set apart for service to lead the faithful in their common life and witness. Saint Augustine said it best: "When I am frightened by what I am for you, I am consoled by what I am with you. For you, I am a bishop, with you I am a Christian. The former designates an office, the latter, grace. The former spells danger, the latter, salvation."[32]

VII. The Trinity As a Theological Construct for Ministry.

One could make a case for the claim that the theological concept of the trinity is the single most uniquely Christian doctrine. The word trinity is not of course found in Scripture, and the doctrinal formulations took several hundred years of theological development. Furthermore, in a rationalist age the notion of a trinity would seem to demand a kind of intellectual gymnastics to explain and defend a belief that is most often perceived as alien to reason.

But perhaps for these very reasons rather than in spite of them, I find myself drawn to the power of the concept of the trinity as the defining Christian doctrine. While its primary purpose is to say something about our understanding of God, it is also a useful metaphor by which to measure the adequacy of other areas of faith and life. The relevant question here is whether it is a useful construct to interpret an understanding of ministry in and for the church. How might the minister be understood as the representative of the triune God?[33]

---

[31]See diagram at the end of this essay on authority and power in ministry which seeks to graphically express the relationship of person and office for effective ministry.

[32]Quoted by Gisbert Greshake in *The Meaning of Christian Priesthood* (Dublin: Four Courts Press Ltd., 1982, Translated, 1988), p. 100.

[33]George H. Williams interprets the development of threefold ministry in the Ante-Nicene period in relationship to the developing understandings of the trinity. For

22

Is it possible within an Anabaptist faith to in any way claim the minister as having a spiritual role that serves in some manner as the representative of God? That is the heart of the question. Or might the question be nuanced in another way: is it possible for the Mennonite minister to function as God's representative in behalf of the church? What are the theological risks in making such a claim? What are the theological and spiritual benefits in venturing near the borders of heresy?

If we speak of God the Father[34] as the *persona* of God's transcendent presence in our world, wrapped in awe and mystery, how shall we understand the minister in any way fulfilling that place in the congregation? On the one hand we call for the minister to be fully transparent, meaning that there must be honesty and openness if there is to be authenticity and integrity to serve effectively. But powerful ministry may also embrace a hidden dimension in which the person is never fully known, in which there resides within the pastoral self a quality that is inviting by the very richness of what is never fully perceived or understood but which we have always ascribed to as "spiritual depth of character."

If we speak of Jesus the Christ as the *persona* of God's historic presence in the world, offering his words and his work as the sacrificial and liberating action for our salvation, how shall those who minister in his name incorporate into their ministry dimensions of the same? Here we must reclaim again the servanthood image to which Jesus himself so clearly pointed as the essential defining quality of leadership.[35] The redemptive quality of sacrificial service by those who serve in ministry today is in grave danger of being lost and forgotten, in part a victim of an equally necessary sense of being professional.

---

instance, he quotes Ignatius of Antioch. "In his role of chief pastor of the flock, the bishop is the type of God and specifically of God the Father." A century and a half later the Syrian canon law, the *Didascalia*, says that "the bishop sits for you in the place of God Almighty." *The Ministry in Historical Perspective*, H. Richard Niebuhr and Daniel D. Williams, eds. (New York: Harper and Brothers, 1956), pp. 30, 54.

[34]What to do about gender-specific language today is problematic, especially with a trinitarian tradition that has identified the first person of the Trinity with such a gender-specific term?

[35]Mark 10:42-45.

If we speak of the Spirit as the *persona* of God's contemporary presence in the world, inspiring, comforting, and energizing the church, how shall those who must live and serve in an imperfect world and with an imperfect church be themselves inspired, comforted, and energized by that same Spirit to authentically represent God's presence among us? Ministry is today and it will be tomorrow. It is lived in the reality of the present time and the present world. While ministry reaches out to embrace the past and the future, it does so always with the goal of bringing to bear the true prophetic and apocalyptic word of God to the contemporary reality of the church.

There is another way in which we might probe the relevance of the trinity as a foundation for our theology of ministry and that has to do with the threefold ministry tradition, often interpreted as the tradition of the bishop, the tradition of the elder,[36] and the tradition of the deacon.[37]

This threefold tradition which we can observe in its embryo form in the New Testament came to fuller expression by the end of the first century. Ignatius is the first to make reference to the threefold ministry within one context: "Avoid divisions, as the beginning of evil. Follow, all of you, the bishop, as Jesus Christ followed the Father; and follow the presbytery (elders) as the Apostles. Moreover, reverence the deacons as the commandment of God."[38] This threefold ministry continues to re-emerge time and again in church history, giving evidence to the church's strong need for oversight, pastoral leadership in the congregation, and some form of lay ministry that is rooted close to the people. It has formed the foundation of ministry within Mennonite history and is again being reclaimed for the church of the future.[39]

---

[36]The term elder is exceedingly problematic in Mennonite usage, inasmuch as it has been used as the definitive term for all three forms of the threefold ministry tradition. At the present time, its most prevalent usage, especially with the Mennonite Church, is in the third form of ministry or the equivalent of the deacon.

[37]See the World Council of Churches document on the "Theology of Ministry" in *Baptism, Eucharist, and Ministry (Geneva: World Council of Churches, 1982).*

[38]*A New Eusebius*, J. Stevenson, ed. (New York: The Macmillan Company, 1957), p. 48.

[39]See the Joint Leadership Polity document which is presently under development; it strongly reaffirms the vitality of the threefold ministry tradition, one that is valuable and necessary for the well-being of the church.

While there is nothing magical in the number three that would tie together the Trinity and the threefold ministry tradition, there may be more than coincidence here. For instance, the essential unity of the trinity would help us to maintain the essential unity and oneness that must exist within the threefold ministry if it is to serve effectively.

While it may push the point to suggest that the bishop represents God the Father, there is an enduring sense of relationship between transcendence and the requirements of oversight that are the bishop's special responsibility.

While the pastor can never confuse his/her role within the church as its savior and lord (there is but one Savior and one Lord, Jesus of Nazareth, the Christ of God), there is an incarnational presence within the congregation that accurately must describe the pastor's reality.

While the deacon (elder) will seldom be mistaken for the Holy Spirit, there is a parallel work of counseling and consoling that should not be missed or ignored.

Thus, might the trinity as a normative Christian doctrine be perceived as useful in testing the adequacy of our developing theology of ministry.

V. Conclusion

When I began to seriously reflect on a theology for ministry in 1991, I put down for my own instruction a series of fourteen points which seemed then to be significant in the process of recovering, rethinking, and re-imagining issues in a Mennonite theology for Christian ministry. As one test whether that goal has been achieved in an initial way, let me conclude by listing these fourteen elements.

1. It should be linked with a theology of the church and its ministry. Pastoral ministry does not exist outside of the church. All forms of ministry, including ministry in specialized settings, must be rooted in our theology of the church. But that understanding of the church must be rooted both in idealistic forms – the church as the body of Christ, and in its reality – the church as institution.

2. The theology of ministry should have trinitarian linkages, expressing the transcendent presence of God, the historical presence of God in Christ, and the contemporary presence of God in the Spirit.

3. It must grow out of an authority systems model that takes seriously the combined effect of Scripture – both Old and New Testaments, of Christian

tradition – both ecumenical and Anabaptist, and the living experience of those in the practice of ministry.

4. It must be broad enough to cover ministry within the church – congregation – and ministry as mission in the world.

5. It must be focused enough to helpfully differentiate between what the church has traditionally referred to as laity and clergy. If these terms are not acceptable, we must find alternative ways to speak about this differentiation.

6. It must reflect the dialectical - dialogical or bi-polar tensions that exist between such elements as church/world, faith/doubt, salvation/judgment, priest/prophet, symbol/reality, servant/leader, roles/functions, good/evil, and ideal/reality. As examples, these reflect the inevitable and necessary ambiguity of ministry.

7. It must undergird ministry with overarching concepts, as opposed to undermining ministry with overbearing slogans.

8. It must be shaped by those in the practice of ministry alongside of and in collegial partnership with the academy of ministry, our seminaries.

9. It must incorporate understandings of the self, including the complementary gifts of being and doing as well as understandings of the church's office of ministry and the symbolic roles lived out through that office. It must link the self and the office in symbiotic relationships for effective ministerial functions to flow from the self and the office.

10. It must help us to more clearly define the specific tasks of ministry including *kerygma* – preaching; *didaskalos* – teaching; *apostello* – witness; and *koinonia* – community building.

11. It should speak to the issues of schism, heresy, orthodoxy, and order; it should assist the church in understanding the role of leadership for appropriate and necessary boundary maintenance and structures of accountability.

12. It should link to the historic threefold ministry tradition which has emerged and re-emerged time and again in Christian history.

13. It ought to define ministry with the orders of redemption rather than with the orders of perfection, so that ministry itself might authentically reflect the human condition that we are always "wounded healers" and "treasure in clay jars."

14. It must interpret and defend the concerns for inclusiveness and equality within the church so that ministry is as inclusive as the Christian gospel in which "there is no longer Jew or Greek, there is no longer slave or free, there is no longer male and female; for all of you are one in Christ Jesus" (Galatians 3:28).

AUTHORITY FOR MINISTRY

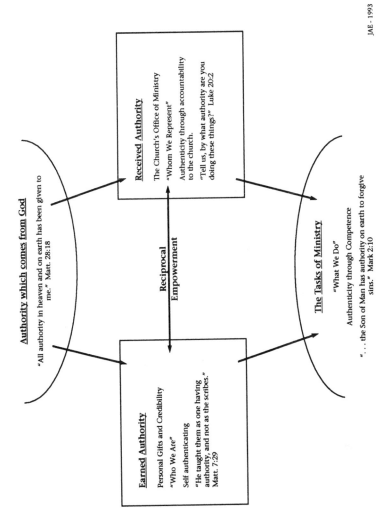

Authority which comes from God

"All authority in heaven and on earth has been given to me." Matt. 28:18

Received Authority

The Church's Office of Ministry

"Whom We Represent"

Authenticity through accountability to the church.

"Tell us, by what authority are you doing these things?" Luke 20:2

Reciprocal Empowerment

Earned Authority

Personal Gifts and Credibility

"Who We Are"

Self authenticating

"He taught them as one having authority, and not as the scribes." Matt. 7:29

The Tasks of Ministry

"What We Do"

Authenticity through Competence

". . . the Son of Man has authority on earth to forgive sins." Mark 2:10

JAE - 1993

Chapter Two

Helping Dreams Come True:
Toward Wholeness – Articulating the Vision

Erick Sawatzky

This presentation was originally given at the Brethren and Mennonite Chaplains annual meeting in Nashville, Tennessee, February 27, 1990.

I. Introduction

I want to begin by weaving together several experiences, Scriptures, stories, and musings. If you are of an analytical bent, you may wonder what these have to do with each other. If you are an intuitive person, you may find commonality.

The first is a reflection on my ten years as a congregational pastor. Without trying to brag too much, I was by common standards a successful pastor. I worked hard, sometimes long hours, sacrificed family time, attended many committee meetings, offered occasional creative ideas, got involved with the youth, was elected to community and conference boards and committees, and, to borrow Eugene Peterson's words, became adept enough at creative plagiarism to develop a bit of a reputation for intelligence.

I learned enough appropriate voice control for preaching, praying, and counseling to convince people of my sincerity. I became efficient enough at office management, so as to convince people that I was both on top of things and a very busy pastor. Yes, I projected an acceptable image to most people.

While I know that one cannot fool all of the people all of the time, and I really did not intend to fool anybody, I do feel that I did fool some of the people some of the time, either intentionally or unintentionally. I know I took some solace in a comment from a pastoral colleague who once said something like, "I choose more often to do something than to pray about it."

The second musing comes from Anne Tyler's novel *Morgan's Passing*, and is reported by Eugene Peterson in *Working the Angles*.[1] Tyler tells the story of a middle-aged Baltimore man who passed through people's

---

[1] Eugene Peterson, *Working the Angles* (Grand Rapids: Eerdmans, 1987), pp. 5-6.

lives with astonishing aplomb and expertise in assuming roles and gratifying expectations.

The novel opens with Morgan watching a puppet show on a church lawn on a Sunday afternoon. A few minutes into the show, a young man came from behind the puppet stage and asked, "Is there a doctor here?" After thirty or forty seconds of silence in the audience, Morgan stood up slowly, and deliberately approached the young man and asked, "What is the trouble?" The puppeteer's pregnant wife is in labor. A birth seems imminent. Morgan put the young couple in the back of his station wagon and set off for Johns Hopkins Hospital.

Halfway there the husband cried, "The baby is coming!" Morgan, calm and self-assured, pulled to the curb, sent the about-to-be father to the corner for a Sunday paper as a substitute for towels and bed sheets, and delivered the baby. He then drove to the emergency room of the hospital, put the mother and baby safely on a stretcher, and disappeared.

After the excitement died down, the couple asked for Dr. Morgan. They want to thank him. However, no one had ever heard of a Dr. Morgan. The couple were puzzled and frustrated that they couldn't express their gratitude. Several months later they were pushing their baby in a stroller and saw Morgan walking on the other side of the street. They ran over to greet him, showing him the healthy baby that he brought into the world. They told him how hard they had looked for him and of the hospital's bureaucratic incompetence in tracking him down.

In an unaccustomed gush of honesty, he admitted to them that he was not really a doctor. In fact, he ran a hardware store. But they needed a doctor, and being a doctor in those circumstances was not all that difficult. "It is an image thing," he told them. "You discern what people expect and fit into it. You can get by with it in all the honored professions."

Morgan had been doing this all of his life – impersonating doctors, lawyers, pastors, and counselors as occasions presented themselves. Then he confided, "You know, I would never pretend to be a plumber or impersonate a butcher. They would find me out in twenty seconds."

A third story. When I left the congregational pastorate and became the executive director of the Pastoral Institute and a prison chaplain in Saskatoon, there were many changes in my life. And people would ask me about these. For the most part I didn't mind. But the question that I was often asked, and the question that cut the deepest and hurt the most was, "Why did you leave the ministry?" I don't know how you have responded when people have asked you that question, but somehow my system would wince, almost like someone had cut a cardboard box with a butcher's knife. Strange, no one has asked me that about coming to teach at the seminary.

Let me put this in the context of a scriptural text from 2 Corinthians 4:16-18. "Therefore we do not lose heart. Though outwardly we are wasting away, yet inwardly we are being renewed day by day. For our light and momentary troubles are achieving for us an eternal glory that far outweighs them all. So we fix our eyes not on what is seen, but on what is unseen. For what is seen is temporary, but what is unseen is eternal."

I realize that experiences, anecdotes, and Scriptures can lead us in many directions, some helpful and some not helpful, some spectacular and some unspectacular. What I want to express to us this afternoon, however, is, in my opinion, something very simple and unspectacular – and that is that the dream of chaplaincy is basically the same dream as any other Christian ministry, and that is "to help others, through words, acts and relationships, to experience as fully as possible the reality of God's presence and love in their lives."[2] This is not a new dream. Rather, I suggest it is a dream that has sustained ministry through the ages.

To flesh out that dream, I want to focus our attention on: (1) the context of the pastoral chaplain's dream, and (2) the heart of the dream itself.

II. The Context of the Dream

In what kind of a world do we minister? What is the mind-set and frame of reference of people in our day? This varies with people, of course, but I believe it is a common assumption among western Christians that we are more broad-minded today than people in years past. We think that we are more aware of our world and better informed. Yes, our horizons have expanded from a once narrow parochialism to the global and beyond – even the universe. In school we were taught about the barbarians, the dark ages, and the accompanying bondage of superstition and petty feudal kingdoms of medieval Europe.

We were rescued from all this. We were taught by the renaissance and the age of reason, commonly called the enlightenment. This was dubbed "the best of all possible worlds" at the time. But even that was not enough: and so more recently we have been led to drink at the fountain of the here and

---

[2]Lawrence E. Holst, *Hospital Ministry* (New York: Crossroads, 1985), p. 46.

now – feeling good, self-realization, self-actualization, and individualism, assured by our culture that this surely and truly is ultimate freedom and the salvation for which we were created. We have arrived.

There is, however, a less popular and much more sober assessment of our history and of our contemporary context of life, as well as our salvation. Herbert O'Driscoll,[3] speaking to us about life in our time, has reminded us that from the perspective of religious faith, we have not moved from darkness to light or from the minuscule to the grandiose, but in the opposite direction. We have, in successive stages, boxed God into smaller and smaller compartments of our life and awareness, to where now God belongs only in the Sunday morning worship service – and some of us wonder sometimes whether God is even allowed there anymore. O'Driscoll reminds us that God once belonged in the universe of travel, but sea travelers like Magellan, Columbus, and others demythologized that realm as travel and navigation came under the control of humans. God once belonged in astronomy and physics, but Copernicus and Galileo were instrumental in making discoveries that allowed humans to remove God from those sciences. Medicine and healing was once the domain of the transcendent; God was the great healer. But with modern, technical, and scientific discoveries about bacteria, medications, etc., and with sophisticated machines, surgical methods, and now transplants and genetic engineering, God has all too often been removed from the healing world as well.

Our time, O'Driscoll reminds us, is an apocalyptic time. It is a time of great uncertainty, a time when the present seems ripped away from the past, a time of great ambiguity when there seems to be a great chasm between present reality and a meaningful tomorrow. In fact, one of the characteristics of an apocalyptic time is the uncertainty of whether there will be a tomorrow. He says that living in our time is like standing on a beach after the tide has gone out. All around us lays the wreckage of the past – as far as we can see. We see past glorious civilizations; we see economic and industrial paradises; we see spiritual and philosophical peaks – but they are now all in ruin. The tide has gone out and neither you nor I nor anyone else is sure whether the tide will come in again, and if it does, what will it bring with it. All seems uncertain. There seem to be no sure answers. Many look at the past with regret and guilt and at the future with fear and dread.

---

[3]Herbert O'Driscoll, in an address given at the annual meeting of the Saskatoon Pastoral Institute, May 30, 1985.

Peter Erb, from Wilfrid Laurier University, speaking on the topic "The Death of Spirituality in the Modern World,"[4] reminds us that through the lenses of spirituality too, we live in perilous times; and the present revival of spirituality is not all it is hyped up to be – and not that encouraging. Too often, present-day spirituality focuses on a type of interiority very foreign to Christian tradition, and all too cozy with Eastern transcendentalism – the assumptions of modern individualism and of self-psychology. Erb's point is that the spiritual horizons of Western Christians have been successfully narrowed since the Reformation and not broadened.

With the demise of Christendom in the Reformation era and following, people began to think more narrowly. For example, instead of coming from or identifying themselves with the vast world of Christendom, people began to identify with a geographical and political region like Saxony, which may have been Lutheran. Or again in England, Henry VIII became the defender of the Church of England – a geographical region. Then in the eighteenth century, with the Enlightenment and the French Revolution, the political began to give way to the personal and the individual, which more recently in our day has been giving way to the self.

Paralleling this narrowing in the spiritual and religious realm, Erb argues, Christianity moved from a broad emphasis on the Father or the creative principle of the Trinity to an emphasis on the Son, a personal salvation emphasis; and now it appears that we are moving to an even narrower emphasis on the Spirit and personal experience. And so our world views have moved from the very broad to the rather narrow and individualistic.

The point that I am wanting to establish is that you and I are ministering to people whose religious, spiritual horizons may be very fragile, very limited, very narrow. In fact, narrowness might not be the best image to project, because narrowness assumes some continuity. My personal experience and my encounter with others is that religious and spiritual realities are experienced more like disconnected dots, little islands in the sea of life, rather than a connected, narrow chain.

Furthermore, in order to feed their desperate craving for spiritual meaning, people in our day shop at the religious supermarkets that abound. And so this disconnected spiritual island gets fed with a religious package

---

[4]Peter Erb, in an address at the Associated Mennonite Biblical Seminary, "A Fire Put Out: The Death of Spirituality in the Modern World," May 6, 1987.

from the home church, another disconnected island gets fed from the Crystal Cathedral, another from the therapist, and still another from New Age thinking, and a fifth from silent meditation, and so on and so forth. People fill spaces with science, pseudo science, superstition, the horoscope, and what have you. What is missing as individuals cast about for meaning is coherence, connectedness, and comprehensiveness. And this is not only the case for prison inmates and folks who grew up outside of Brethren and Mennonite communities. These folks are also staunch Brethren and Mennonites who have been in church all their lives.

It is in this context that we are called to a pastoral vision and to a ministry. As we encounter our people in our churches, our hospitals, our retirement centers, our special care homes, and on our streets, we have to decide what kind of ministry we are going to have. Will we fall into line with broad-based cultural expectations? Will we become entrepreneurs in the religious supermarket chain, offering people a vast array of choices of how to meet their many spiritual needs? Will we buy into the cultural success models of ministry, or the professionalized client pay-as-you-get-saved model? It is helpful to remember that apocalyptic times are also times of opportunity and creativity. I am proposing this afternoon that the dream toward wholeness – the pastoral vision – is different than narrowly defined professionalism or the corporate sales manager in the religious supermarket.

III. The Pastoral Vision

What then is the pastoral vision? I am proposing this afternoon that the chaplain's pastoral vision, like the congregational pastor's pastoral vision, is a vision for deepened spiritual connectedness with God through Christ in all of its dimensions. This means first of all a ministry of prayer and spiritual direction that is rooted in a life of prayer and contemplation of the minister her/himself.

I am not, today, going to attempt to outline what form such a life should take. Nor am I suggesting in any way that there is any one form of spirituality or spiritual discipline. I am only wanting to assert the point that we as ministers find it all too easy to get so wrapped up in our ministering activity that we lose our own spiritual center. We forget or become too lazy to pray.

Urban T. Holmes writes,

> The ancient sin of acedia (spiritual boredom) lies at the root of the pastor's or priest's refusal to heed the calling to be the instrument of spiritual growth. . . . The fact is that many ordained persons quickly lose a sense of the excitement of the spiritual quest. They succumb to acedia in those forms that are to a degree peculiar to our times. American religion is obsessed with the 'warm sins' such as illicit sex and gluttony; the sins that should concern us far more deeply are those that prevent the ordained from ever exercising their spiritual vocation. These 'cold sins' truly violate the mission of the pastor to be a symbol, symbol bearer, and hermeneut. They arise not from an excess of passion, but from a fear of passion. They are the product of a calculated apathy, sustained only by the embers of a dying soul."[5]

It is all too easy to lose Jesus in the temple. The first part of the vision, then, is to keep our eyes on God in Christ, the center of our ministry.

The second point is to rethink the meaning of success as it relates to ministry. I am sure that you, like I, have seen book titles and read articles with titles like "The Successful Church" or "The Successful Pastor." These are attractive to us because all of us like to succeed. And we like to succeed the easy way. Our culture models success. It models it in terms of bigness, beauty, control, independence, wealth, and doing it "my way."

We do well to remember, however, that Christian ministry is first and foremost God's ministry and not our own. Christian ministry is rooted in God's reconciling and saving work in the world. Our focus as God's agents is to pass on that reconciling message and help persons experience that loving and reconciling relationship with God. This is primarily the work of the Holy Spirit. Therefore, words like success and failure really have very little place in our discussion – faithfulness and disobedience, perhaps, but hardly success and failure. Success and failure language is business language. It attracts business-type thinking and business techniques. I am not against business. I just do not believe that business language and business symbols are the best

---

[5]Urban T. Holmes, *Spirituality for Ministry* (San Francisco: Harper and Row, 1982), pp. 42-43.

way to think and speak about ministry. They fail at the point that they offer us only measurable guides to success and failure.

Thirdly, the pastoral vision has to do with rethinking the meaning of ordination and calling to ministry. I want to assert that the threat to Mennonite pastoral ministry and Mennonite and Brethren chaplaincy in the last thirty years has not only come from growing secularism and business language; it has not only come from escalating health-care costs, budget cuts, difficult administrators, or the threat from the apocalyptic nature of our time, though all of these may to some extent be true.

An equal threat to our ministry, I believe, has come from an over interpretation of selected biblical texts like Ephesians 4, Acts 4, Romans 12, and Titus 1 and an overinterpretation of selected Anabaptist themes like servanthood, community, and priesthood of all believers, to the point where meaningful leadership, pastoral identity, and yes, pastoral functioning has been difficult if not impossible for many.

I suppose that statement requires some elaboration. Let me attempt an explanation. There was a time in our not-too-distant history as Mennonites and Brethren when we knew who ministers were and what ministers did. The patterns varied somewhat from one geographical region to another across the United States and Canada. But whether it was being chosen by lot, being nominated and voted on by the membership, or whether it had to do with a slightly different cut of the coat, a broader brimmed hat, a limited preaching ministry, a diakonal service ministry, or overseeing ministry as a bishop or an *aeltester*, identity was fairly clear. The point is that in those situations and contexts, the broad membership as well as the chosen and ordained knew their identity – who they were, whose they were, who they were to be, and how they were to act and function. Subject to abuse? Yes. Imperfect? Of course!

Then came the 1950s and 1960s: more education, more professionalization, the theological and sociological critique of the church by the erudite Concern Movement, the premiere years of the recovery of the Anabaptist vision, antiestablishment and antileadership thinking, and a new set of words around ministry – servanthood, enabler, equipper, facilitator, and yes, priesthood of all believers. These were the words around ministry when I was a seminary student in 1969-73, along with covenant community and koinonia groups. Shared ministry, team ministry, and co-pastoring were not yet so much in vogue. In Church and Ministry class, we talked about everyone being a minister. "No one is not a minister" was the slogan. What we could not talk about was pastoral identity, the pastoral office, pastoral presence, leadership, power, authority, ordination, or, for that matter, the pastorate – which is different from speaking about the function of pastoring.

Clearly this is not the occasion to argue the academic fine points of a universal-functional versus an office-vocational view of ministry. We'll leave that for the seminary classroom and the journals. But my vision and dream for ministry, whether that is in a congregational setting or as a chaplain in another institutional setting, is obviously grounded in a more office-vocational centered view than the functional-universal understanding. (I have a rather simplistic view of that office versus function debate. It seems impossible to me to equip anyone else for ministry without modeling what that ministry is. Therefore, office and function are inseparable.)

I want to assert, therefore, that the vision for chaplaincy and the vision for ministry in Brethren and Mennonite circles is served best by an appreciated understanding of ordination rather than a depreciated view.

Clearly, language gets sticky here and it is easy to say the wrong thing or to say the right thing poorly. But my central point is that pastoral ministry and chaplaincy can and will only be affirmed and appreciated in our circles (by our institutions, administrators, and our people – and sometimes I am convinced our people understand it best) if we understand and accept the significance of the calling out, the credentialling of, and yes, the ordination of select persons to the vocation of ministry – not only to a specific function or task.

In talking chaplaincy we are talking about a calling and a vocation – a ministry calling and a ministry vocation just as surely as we talk about a congregational pastoral calling and vocation. Chaplaincy is not to be understood by the denomination and by the public as a narrow task, as a second-rate expression of ministry reserved for those who could not make it in the congregation, or at the seminary, or with the denominational office. Chaplaincy is not to be viewed as a partial ministry void of real integrity, accountability, and prophetic vision. Rather, what we are looking for in chaplaincy is the full acceptance, the full membership, with accountability, into that Mennonite and Brethren "Order of Ministry" – which I know does not officially exist but which does unofficially exist in the hearts, minds, and attitudes of the public, the church, and the church hierarchy.

For this to happen we need to appreciate and accept a theology of ministry which embraces ministry as vocation, as a high calling, as office, just as much as it embraces a theology of ministry as servanthood and function.

Only when chaplains are understood as full ministers can and will conference ministers and the central offices include chaplains in their thinking, in their programming, and in their pastoral care. And only then will we stop asking, "Why did you leave the ministry?" Only when chaplains are understood as full ministers can they be instrumental in mediating signs of grace and symbols of forgiveness, acceptance, and love to persons in need.

Fourthly, the pastoral vision appreciates the ministry of presence. Every chaplain knows the importance of the ministry of presence. There are many occasions when there is simply nothing that can be said or done to be helpful. All you can do is be there. But the ministry of presence is heavily dependent upon embracing ministry as vocation and calling.

As a prison chaplain in the Saskatoon Correctional Center a few years ago, I found myself faced with a dilemma. My task was not only to be a chaplain, but since this was a new institution, my task was to establish the chaplaincy tradition there and to model what the chaplaincy presence would be in that place in the future. I soon discovered that I had several models to choose from. One was the soul-winning preacher model – the one who would preach rousing and convicting sermons to guilt-ridden prisoners, or invite others who could do this better than I could in the faith that someone would raise their hand and say "Yes" to Jesus when the invitation was given. This was modeled for me by the traveling ex-con-now-hero evangelist and by fundamentalist groups in town.

Another was the professional religionist model – the one who held or led religious services and was the keeper or dean of the chapel and was the proper presence on ceremonial occasions. Occasionally this person might meet people.

Still a third model was that of the advocate or the change agent – the one who set out to change the correctional system into something more humane and decent, or perhaps in grandiose moments even dream of abolishing the whole system.

Somehow none of these appealed to me as adequate models. The soul-winning model seemed to me like "hit and run." The sacramental, professional religionist model was too formal and distant and not at all congruent with who I was or what I sensed prisoners needed. Advocacy simply took too long. Besides, the correctional system did not need change as much as it needed abolition. I chose, instead, a ministry of presence with people.

A helpful descriptive metaphor for me was Henry Nouwen's title, *"The Living Reminder."*[6] It seemed to me that the only way I could lead any religious services, preach with any integrity, or be an advocate for inmates was if I walked where they walked, sat where they sat, listened to their stories, sometimes wept with them in their grief, all in the spirit of Jesus. This was on the assumption that perhaps, just perhaps, the only Bible they would ever read, the only Gospel they would ever hear, and the only grace they might ever experience was some living representative, some living reminder of Jesus Christ. Presumptuous? Perhaps. Nevertheless, this seemed and still seems right to me. It is so easy to insulate ourselves from the real needs. It is so easy to become so busy running the programs that ministry to people gets lost. And perhaps Jesus gets lost too.

Yes, every baptized Christian is, in the broadest understanding of the term, a minister. But ministry and chaplaincy ministry are also a vocation and a calling which makes possible the ministry of presence and, hence, is more than the sum of its functions and tasks, just as the symphony is more than the sum of individual notes, or a painting is more than a combination of colors.

Fifthly, the pastoral vision includes a subversive dimension. There is something subversive about a pastoral vision or dream that relies more on being than on doing frantic activity, more on spiritual direction and prayer and presence than statistics and programs, and more on the Word than on our many words.

I realize that the word subversive conjures up negative images for many of us, and on the first bounce we might say, "No, that's not right." But I rather like the word and the concept. It's the mustard seed idea, the yeast concept, or in the apostle Paul's language, "When I am weak, then I am strong."

There is a classic line in the South African film entitled "Cry Freedom" when Steven Biko, referring to the Soweto school situation, says, "Change the way people think and you never know what will happen." That, brothers and sisters, is much of what the gospel of reconciliation is all about – not departments, not programs, not the number of services held, but changing the way people think – from narrow thinking to broader thinking, from disconnectedness to connectedness, from despair to hope, from unbelief to faith, from judgment to grace, and from hatred to love. We do this through

---

[6]Henri J. M. Nouwen, *The Living Reminder* (New York: The Seabury Press, 1977).

prayer, presence, touch, rituals, the written and proclaimed Word. And when we do that, we are never sure what will happen next.

I hope we all understand this is not passive pastoring, mystical ministry, chummy chaplaincy, or whatever alliteration we create. This is real and hard work. And while I am not suggesting it will be empirically justifiable, that it will build a strong and numerically large department, that it will help balance the budget, or that it will convince a doubting administrator, I do believe it is authentic ministry. And it is the only kind of ministry that I know of that leads toward true wholeness. And if it is authentic, if it leads to wholeness, if it is really true, then ministry will have a meaningful future.

CMC Resource Centre

CONFERENCE OF MENNONITES IN CANADA
600 Shaftesbury Blvd. Winnipeg, MB, R3P 0M4
888-0781 ● 1-800-665-1954 (outside Manitoba) ● FAX: 831-5675

Chapter Three

Ministerial Status and the Theology of Ministry

Rodney J. Sawatsky

> Rodney Sawatsky has spoken and written about ministerial polity and theology in a number of contexts. This article is the text of a paper he presented at the Conference Based Theological Education Directors/Adjunct Faculty Consultation, November 5, 1987, at Conrad Grebel College in Waterloo, Ontario.

I do not come to this topic as an expert. Even though I've had opportunities to speak to leadership and authority issues, I still feel very much like a dilettante. But I am very interested and concerned about the topic, and since I have a platform I'm ready to preach. Before we get into some problem areas that need our consideration, I should make several introductory comments.

The problems the Mennonite church faces in this area are not unique. Most of our questions regarding leadership are shared by many other denominations and even the larger society. We still need to focus on the particular manifestations and potential solutions relevant to our situation, but we should not lose sight of the larger context. In fact, by comparison the Mennonite church is relatively strong; therefore, our mood should be one of thankfulness and optimism.

The analysis some of us are making regarding our present situation is not shared by everyone. There are those among us who are at least as committed and insightful who would propose different analyses and solutions. Accordingly, we need to work with humility. But we need to discuss and debate both the theoretical and practical levels of ministry without closing the door prematurely by simply saying "that's not biblical" or "that's not Anabaptist."

I. Status Crisis for Ministers

Moving to our analysis, I want to begin with the place and role of the minister in our churches and society. My sense is that since the "Sixties" and for some denominations much earlier, Protestants (as well as the Roman Catholics and others) have witnessed a growing sense of uncertainty as to the place and role of the Christian minister. We have experienced this in terms of the debate about the legitimacy of professional ministry, the questions surrounding the meaning of ordination, the inadequate process for releasing ministers, and the difficulty of attracting some of our more gifted persons to consider ministry.

There are undoubtedly many ways to understand this phenomenon and I've made my own attempts before. Here I would like to suggest another angle, namely, what Richard Hofstadter has called a "status revolution" or "status crisis." He utilized this interpretative category in his analysis of late nineteenth-century American progressivism:

> The clergy were probably the most conspicuous losers from the status revolution. They not only lost ground in all the outward ways, as most middle-class elements did, but were also hard hit in their capacity as moral and intellectual leaders by the considerable secularization that took place in American society and intellectual life in the last three decades of the nineteenth century.
>
> In the light of this situation, it may not be unfair to attribute the turning of the clergy toward reform and social criticism not solely to their disinterested perception of social problems and their earnest desire to improve the world, but also to the fact that as persons who were in their own way suffering from the incidence of the status revolution they were able to understand and sympathize with the problems of other disinherited groups. The increasingly vigorous interest in the social gospel, so clearly manifested by the clergy after 1890, was in many respects an attempt to restore through secular leadership some of the spiritual influence and authority and social prestige that clergymen had lost through the upheaval in the system of status and the secularization of society.[1]

Ramsey Cook, a Canadian historian, recently argued similarly in *The Regenerators*:

---

[1]Richard Hofstadter, *The Age of Reform* (New York: Vintage Books, 1955), pp. 150-151.

42

There was further and perhaps even fatal weakness in the strategy that substituted sociology for theology. Theology, the science of religion, had historically provided clergymen and the church with a recognized place in society. Theology to the clergy was what medical science was to the physician, knowledge of the law to the lawyer, and disciplined learning to the teacher. "Abandoning theology," Ann Douglas has written, echoing Goldwin Smith: "the minister lost his expertise in the realm of what the Psalmist called 'God's thoughts'; he was inevitably forced to seek the lowest common denominator in the minds of his listeners: some loosely defined preoccupation with spiritual, social and personal matters."[2]

My question is: to what extent is the Mennonite ministry experiencing a status crisis due to a loss of subject matter, that is, a loss of a unique area of expertise? Let me explain this question in three ways.

First, I wonder to what extent we have lost the understanding that the human being is essentially a spiritual being – that she is body, mind, and soul. And I wonder to what extent beginning in the "Sixties" with the growing emphasis on the with the growing emphasis on the church's responsibility for social change ministers saw their message focused on the body and mind rather than on the soul. Or even when supposedly speaking holistically, the soul got lost in body and mind. Did the focus on social issues and psychological needs de-emphasize the human person as spirit? To what extent they were caught in the mood of the times or to what extent ministers themselves created this situation is difficult to determine. Was this perhaps seen to be the only way to get a hearing, to be relevant, to maintain social status?

Whatever the cause, it seems to me that theology (the study of God) and *Seelsorge* (the care for souls) lost some of their status as our anthropology narrowed to body and mind. Apparently secular society cannot understand anyone specializing in the world of the soul, and I wonder if this assumption has also influenced Christian ministry negatively. But this is, after all, the area of the minister's unique if not exclusive expertise. With a limited anthropology comes a limited theology and finally a loss of a unique calling for a Christian minister. Or the reverse – the place and role of the minister

[2]Ramsey Cook, *The Regenerators: Social Criticism in Late Victorian English Canada* (Toronto: University of Toronto Press, 1985), pp. 230-231.

can only be maintained or regained if they are in an area that people recognize as of vital importance and that no other profession services, if we can speak so crudely!

Secondly, the priesthood of all believers has come to mean that the minister has no unique calling or role. She or he is essentially fulfilling a function and will stay on the job only as long as the performance matches the defined function. For most persons the definition of pastoral function still includes a heavy dose of preaching and counseling which, in turn, is appreciated by many in the congregation and especially among the older is received as authoritative. Yet the question surely haunts the minister: could not or should not others around me do what I am doing because they could do it as well or maybe even better? This is particularly true when theology and the care of souls are de-emphasized in the church in favor of those issues in which the minister may well have less expertise than many others. Surely the status, of if you prefer, the identity of the minister is seriously undermined by some of the ways "the priesthood of all believers" concept is interpreted.

This may be the place to say once again that we need to reexamine the meaning of ordination. If we see the call to ministry as divine and not only human, then ordination is not only to a function but also to an office. Without a renewed sense of ordination, ministry will continue to face a status crisis. Perceiving ordination as merely functional does not make the ministry any less professional; indeed with a richer understanding of ordination, ministry may become something more than just another profession.

On the other hand, why are we so afraid of seeing ministry as a profession? Teaching, social work, law, etc., can all be seen as Christian ministries, yet few would argue that these are not nor should not be professions. Why a double standard in relation to pastoral ministry? It has become for us a profession and will remain so as long as the rest of us are professionalized. Training accordingly should be frankly professional training. This does not mean that other persons should not have theological training; everyone probably should but not everyone will. We live in a world of reality and must program accordingly. We will want to provide theological training for the laity (if we can use that term), but such education should not compromise the specific needs of professional training for professional pastoral ministry.

Thirdly, the place and role of Christian ministry is being influenced negatively, I believe, by the problem of authority in our society. Peter Berger reminds us that pluralism produces relativism, which in turn results in the undermining of all exclusive truth claims, including the messengers of those truth claims. Pluralism reigns in many ways. In biblical studies we recognize a plurality of theologies in the Scriptures. In Anabaptist studies we now speak of polygenesis as well as a plurality of Anabaptist theologies. With such an emphasis on variety, the question inevitably arises: what then is true?

To some extent we have all adopted in some form an understanding of a plurality of truths. We cannot and dare not impose a simple unity where unity does not and cannot exist. Yet we need and want some sense of confidence that truth exists, that there is some order in the chaos. We want some sense of assurance.

Within this relativism the minister is called upon to supply an authoritative center. Yet we are nervous about all authority figures and almost impulsively undermine them. Hence, the minister faces a very delicate balance both in his or her message and his or her personality. Leadership is related to authority. Leadership style and ability are very critical when authority is questioned. To what extent this can be taught I don't know, but I do know that it does need to be learned!

Authority not only needs to be learned but more importantly earned. This is increasingly difficult in the midst of a sophisticated, professionalized community such as we are becoming. It is difficult to differentiate the message and the messenger, thus if the message is to carry authority, so too the messenger will need to be recognized as an authority. It is precisely because of this precarious situation, alongside others we cannot address here, that we need our very best talent entering the ministry.

II. Wanted: A Mennonite Theology for Ministry

We are developing a growing body of fine Mennonite theologians who are working on the question: what should a Mennonite theology look like? This is an important issue, but thus far I'm not sure how much our theologians have helped us in developing a theology for ministry. I'm not saying they have not implicitly done so, but we do need to have this issue addressed directly. What we need and want is a theology of specific relevance and usefulness to the pastoral ministry. In what follows no attempt is made to develop such a theology, but I would like to propose some necessary elements for such a theology.

For one, our theology for ministry must be both positive and inclusively Christian, not narrowly sectarian nor only Mennonite. To a significant extent the theologies developed by protest movements such as Anabaptism are built on negation of and differentiation from others. In the sixteenth-century world where most people were at least nominally Christian, this had a validity that no longer holds in the same way in a twentieth-century secular world. Our task today is to be both more ecumenical and more evangelical, namely, to call people to Christ and to nurture them in the way of Christ together with and not simply over against other Christian churches.

To focus too self-consciously on being Mennonite or Anabaptist or pacifist is not particularly useful in ministry even if it may be in academic theology. This is not to say that these should be de-emphasized but rather simply included in the positive gospel that is preached.

Secondly, our theology for ministry needs to be preachable. The medium and the message are closely related as Marshall McLuhan taught us. Learning how to preach is very important but what to preach is equally important. What does our theology tell us about what to preach and what the place and role of the preached word are? Do we believe that the preacher is the vehicle of God's gracious word to his people? And if so, the what and the how of preaching is very important in a theology for ministry.

Our theology for ministry, thirdly, needs to point us to the transcendent in a world where all has become imminent. A major vehicle to this end is worship. Worship, indeed liturgical renewal, is becoming a major new concern for Mennonites. We have virtually no theology of aesthetics in which, for example, beauty and form and order can be seen to point beyond the mundane to the sacred; we have been iconoclasts primarily.

Yet again in a world where transcendence has eroded, we need to work at regaining a sense of the otherness of God in our worship services. Such worship services will, in turn, sustain us in our services of worship the rest of the week. We can learn from the Anglicans and Pentecostals alike. For both these groups, worship clearly begins with our relationship to God, not to each other. Furthermore, both Anglicans and Pentecostals move beyond the exclusive emphasis on words and thus on the rationality characteristic of Protestantism. We can learn to include the more Catholic and Orthodox appreciation for the symbolic, the mysterious, and the experiential.

Fourthly, our theology for ministry must speak to the body, mind, and soul. Our anthropology and our theology are very close correlates. This for me means learning from the Calvinists and others the important place of the mind, of clear and correct thinking in the life of the Christian. A new emphasis on a theology of creation is needed here. It means continuing to emphasize social ethics, Christian service, and the sharing and caring community that is rich in our tradition.

But especially for the younger generation we need to regain the place of personal ethics alongside social ethics. The category of virtue being re-emphasized by Stanley Hauerwas and others is very valuable here. It also means a new pursuit of spirituality. The Catholics and others have much to teach those of us who tend to think that our activity will save us and the world. Quiet contemplation, devotional reading, prayer, alone and corporately, is absolutely necessary for the well-being not only of our souls but also our bodies and minds.

We could go on with similar analysis, but what does all this mean for our training of ministers? To me it means at least two things. It means that we need to gain clarity as to how one understands ministerial leadership in the Mennonite church. We must respond to the status crisis and that right soon. It means that we need solid professional training. Central to such education is the development of academic programs that directly serve people preparing for the profession of ministerial leadership.

I'm not sure what such professional education would include, but a seminary president told me recently that he is radically redesigning his history courses to make them of direct benefit to congregational ministers, not just for potential college professors. I sense this happening elsewhere, as in the proposal by Hough and Cobb to prepare ministers to be practical theologians.[3]

These are some additional thoughts to those I have shared in other settings on ministerial leadership in Mennonite churches. I hope they may be helpful as the seminary continues to provide us with leadership in the education of ministers.

---

[3]Joseph C. Hough, Jr., and John B. Cobb, Jr. *Christian Identity and Theological Education* (Chico, California: Scholars Press, 1985).

Chapter Four

Inner Call / Inner Ambivalence:
Conflicting Messages in a Fragile Conversation

Renee Sauder

> This presentation was given at the Women in Pastoral Ministry
> Conference on April 26, 1993, in Waterloo, Ontario. It reports on
> an extensive research project concerning the experience of
> Mennonite women in ministry carried out by Renee Sauder on
> behalf of the Mennonite Board of Congregational Ministries.

Last September, Sue Steiner, John Stahl-Wert, Jane Friesen, Janice
Yordy Sutter, and I sat around a table in Elkhart, Indiana, pouring over the
results of the Women in Pastoral Ministry Survey. These persons, who were
functioning as my reference group, had gathered this particular weekend to
help assess and interpret the multitude of numbers and percentages and
comments in this document. Sue had by this time asked me to participate in
this conference, but we had not clearly defined what it was that I would speak
about. It was Saturday morning, and as we talked, an intriguing piece of
information began to come to light.

One of the questions in the survey asked: "How important were each
of the following in your decision to pursue pastoral ministry?" I had listed a
number of possible factors such as: members of your family, the minister of
the church you attended. I wanted to assess what role these external influences
played in a woman's decision to pursue ministry.

But in answer to that question 82 percent of the respondents identified
"inner call" as the most important factor, far outweighing the external factors
related to shoulder tapping or congregational call.

Another question read: "What was the most surprising thing about
being in pastoral ministry?" Now, I had added this question after a
conversation with four women pastors from central Kansas who met with me

to critique the survey instrument. If I remember our conversation correctly, we thought it would be interesting to include such a question, desiring to invite responses about the demands and expectations of the pastoral role. And these kinds of comments I did receive: the difficulty of giving up weekends, the shift from a private to a very public life, the time-consuming nature of being on call twenty-four hours a day.

What I was personally unprepared to read in answer to that question were these statements: "I was surprised that I could do it"; "I was surprised that people liked me . . . that I was considered a good preacher and teacher"; "I was surprised that I was capable of making good decisions . . . that the congregation affirmed me for the gifts I bring to ministry"; "I was surprised by the respect and authority I have received from congregational members."

What was becoming clear to us around the table was that despite the strong sense of inner call that brought women into ministry, women were surprised at discovering their giftedness and adequacy for ministry. Beneath the surface was a deeply acculturated message of inadequacy that left them open to self-doubt regarding their rightful place in ministry and their ability to value the contributions they made as ministering persons.

Recognizing this conflicting message between inner call and inner ambivalence, Sue turned to me from across the table and said, "This is it . . . . this is what I want you to speak to, at the conference in April."

I have been grateful for her suggestion as these months have been an opportunity to probe this inner conversation at a variety of levels. Initially I felt overwhelmed by my colleagues, testimonials of inadequacy and ambivalence. But my reading and research has turned into something of a pilgrimage. I began to understand this tension through my own biography, through the lives of women in my own Mennonite community, and through the stories, experiences, conversations, and voices of women in the Bible. As a resource for our collective journey, I offer these reflections to anyone and to all of us who face and have faced this obstacle.

I. Sources of Our Ambivalence

Except for a few rare individuals among us who make personal commitments, decisions, and vocational choices with unequivocal clarity, most of us ruminate about decisions, envision various considerations in a given situation, or get hung on the horns of ambivalence. The ambivalence that Mennonite women have felt in their call to ministry has, no doubt, a variety of causes. I would like to suggest that this ambivalence be understood through the principles of psychology and the language of discipleship in our theological tradition.

Let me turn then to the field of psychology. What I am about to describe is the experience most commonly expressed by women. It is not meant, however, to generalize about the experience of all women – nor is it meant to deny this experience to men.

The developmental psychologist Erik Erikson states that normal ego development moves from autonomy to relationships. But Nancy Chodorow in her book *The Reproduction of Mothering*[1] and Carol Gilligan in her book *In a Different Voice*[2] shed light upon an entirely different pattern for women.

Because children are primarily parented by women in our culture, a different relational reality forms for girls than for boys. Because of their mothering by women, girls seem to define themselves more in relationship to others. Mothers are more clear about their sons' differences, thus push differentiation. Girls learn identification and bonding. Boys learn otherness and detachment. Young girls develop an early understanding as self-in-relationship rather than self-as-separate, developing an identity that centers not on separation but on connection, and they feel those relationships to be a part of who they are.

Because relationships are so central to a woman's sense of self, a woman's concern is to keep these relationships intact; and thus she strives to be above all else a caring individual. She judges herself on her ability to keep and nurture relationships. Rooted in the web of these relationships, many women find themselves at a disadvantage when they seek to develop an independent voice of their own.

What makes for a healthy self is the ability to choose relatedness as an expression of a strong sense of self rather than as a means to create a sense of self-worth and identity.

Well, what does this analysis have to do with the fragile conversation between call and ambivalence? In her provocative book *Can Women Reimage*

---

[1]Nancy Chodorow, *The Reproduction of Mothering: Psychoanalysis and the Sociology of Gender* (Berkeley: University of California Press, 1978).

[2]Carol Gilligan, *In Different Voice: Psychological Theory and Women's Development* (Cambridge: Harvard University Press, 1982).

the Church?[3] Rosemary Chininci suggests that given this view of the self, it is possible for women to experience themselves as connected to and caring for an institution, such as the church, with the same intensity we show toward other people.

Indeed, women in our congregations have loved and cared for the church through a multitude of tasks – teaching Sunday school, serving on its mission committees, preparing fellowship dinners, and organizing vacation Bible school. Many have enjoyed the creative challenge of many aspects of that work. And many have experienced the security of being part of a church community that provides a context for faith and life.

The problem is that the church has not reciprocated with the same care. Women found themselves volunteering many hours of their time, but they had been separated from the policy making and decision making of the church's life. Women had given years of dedicated service in response to the needs of others, fulfilling others' demands; but then they realized that they had been living on the periphery of the church's existence. Women experienced the disharmony of life in the church community where agreement and conformity were paramount. Here they searched for their own voices and identities and vocations while attempting to make a contribution.

How could women begin to claim the call of God on their lives when they ran the risk of hurting others by what would surely be seen as selfish attendance to one's own wants and needs? As women, we have felt conflicted over our desire to offer to the church our potential as ministering persons; at the same time, we have often felt driven back by the ambivalence caused by the deeply ingrained sense of such impropriety. What were women to do with the longing within themselves? Many wondered and agonized. Many confronted the monster of self-doubt.

Few women had the liberty to consider what seemed heresy – to begin to work at the church's center. The Bible had sufficient texts to let us know our role. Our church's tradition was grounded in appropriate places for men and women.

But women were not content to remain on the fringes of the church's life. So our call as women had to come from elsewhere, not because we rejected the Bible and certainly not because we rejected our church tradition.

---

[3]Rosemary Chininci, *Can Women Re-Image the Church?* (New York: Paulist Press, 1992).

It was just that there was no external means of support for the inner longing to say "yes" to God's call on our lives.

One woman wrote: "One day I realized I am accountable to God – not to people – for what God calls me to do." It's not that women wanted to abandon their reliance on outside authority, or abandon the affirmation of the call of the church. It is because that outside authority had remained silent, ignored us, or treated us unfairly that we had to place trust on our inner experience, our own inner truth.

The experience I have just described is reinforced, I think, through the language of discipleship. Lydia Harder, in her article "Discipleship Reexamined: Women in the Hermeneutical Community," suggests that our theological tradition of discipleship, understood primarily as obedience, service, and self-denial, supported the silent role of women, reinforcing the roles that society had assigned to women, functioning to exclude, marginalize, and silence persons in the hermeneutical community. She writes:

> These features of discipleship conformed so closely to the characteristics of women as defined by society that their role was not questioned. A committed disciple was to obey the will of God, that is, to live a life of service and self denial. This implied being humble, giving up power and going the way of the cross. Love, nonresistance, cross bearing, and separation from the world were all part of being disciples. These expectations also coincided with the role of women in a patriarchal society.[4]

I came to consciousness regarding self-denial and self-sacrifice in the attic of my family home. My sister and I would frequent that musty room, rummaging through the piles of old *Life Magazines* and *Reader's Digests*. On this particular afternoon, Kate and I came across a small wooden chest. Inside we found an assortment of oil paints and brushes. That was the day I discovered that my mother was an artist, and that she had given up her interest and considerable talent when she married. She intended to return to her art after the children were raised, but this was not to be, given her untimely death at the age of forty-three. The high premium put on self-denial

---

[4]Lydia Neufeld Harder, "Discipleship Re-Examined: Women in the Hermeneutical Community," *The Church as Theological Community: Essays in Honour of David Schroeder,* Harry Huebner, ed. (Winnipeg, CMBC Publications, 1990), p. 204.

kept her from achieving her full potential as an artist and placed limits on her visual search for creativity.

My mother's story is certainly not unique. Katie Funk Wiebe talks about going through young adult life "believing that it was scriptural to die to self, to become 'nothing' so that Christ could become everything. A Christian had no right to think about self actualization."[5] Certainly for many women, making a choice for oneself would be understood to act against God, opposing the will of God.

This milieu was further reinforced by the hymns we sang in church: "Amazing grace, how sweet the sound, that saved a wretch like me," or "Alas, and did my Savior bleed, And did my Savior die, Would he devote that sacred head, For such a worm as I?"

One can begin to understand the ambivalence that would emerge in this kind of context, in which the secret inner longings and urges to use one's gifts were quelled by the encouragement of a theological tradition that named self-denial and self-sacrifice as a virtue. It has been a difficult journey to take the initiative to overcome this barrier.

One woman wrote in her survey: "My inner call was experienced mostly as a desire not to be phony, to take my Christian life seriously enough, to have an inner life worth giving away and to stop feeling powerless." Do we hang on to old forms in the name of obedience, or do we follow our call to ministry, being willing to follow new light without guilt about what others will say?

If the results of the survey are any indication, the church itself continues to struggle with its own ambivalence regarding the call of women to its ministry. In writing about her ordination experience one woman said: "It took ten years of processing for the congregation to decide whether or not to ordain me. They did ordain me, with the stipulation that I do not preach." This is not an uncommon theme, where congregations define their pastor's role if she is a woman in terms of limitations. Such treatment on the part of congregations does little to encourage an already ambivalent pastoral identity.

The ambivalence of congregations toward women pastors is reflected in the stories of suspicion and curiosity that are so much a part of women's experience. Most of us know what it is like to be treated as a curiosity piece

---

[5]Katie Funk Wiebe, *Our Struggle to Serve: The Stories of Fifteen Evangelical Women*, Virgina Hearn, ed. (Waco, Texas: Word Books, 1979), p. 137.

by those who say things like: "I've never met a woman preacher before . . . I can't believe I finally met one." Or voices at the other end of the phone fall into silence when we identify ourselves as the pastor; Mary Grace Shenk described it in this story:

> The voice on the phone asked: "May I speak to Pastor Shenk, please?" I replied, "This is Pastor Shenk; how may I help you?"
>
> Caller: "You're a woman?" I responded, "Yes, I am." Caller: "Omigod, I must have the wrong number."

II. The Biblical Witness

The content of this presentation is part of larger story. I want to take a few moments to reflect on the stories of biblical women whose responses to God's call may mirror our own experience.

Three visitors come to Abraham's tent one day. Then one of the guests, in disguise, announces that in the spring, Sarah will have a son. The disclosure of the guest's divine identity does not come until Sarah laughs. She laughs in doubt. Not unlike the evening when I was a teenager, and came home from a Mennonite Youth Fellowship gathering and announced to my mother that if I were a man I'd be a preacher. And after the few seconds of silence that followed that announcement, we giggled, doubting the possibility of such a thing. Maybe laughter is faith's companion. Not merely heard at the beginning of salvation history, it remains audible and we hear it in our lives today. Each of our lives contains doubts and detours, high expectations and struggling hopes – the stuff that enables us to begin to live covenant lives together.

We don't know much about the life of the widow at Zarepheth. With a small barley field, she and her son were trying to eke out a frugal living for themselves. When famine struck, she did not know where her next meal could come from to keep the two of them alive. The stranger who appeared at her door one day requested a drink of water and a morsel of bread. Her reply: "As surely as the Lord your God lives, I don't have any bread – only a handful of flour in a jar and a little oil" (1 Kings 17:12).

Elijah told her to make him a small cake of bread – to give what she had. It is a call to faith for a woman who claimed she had nothing to give. Her response of faithfulness did not result in the impoverishment of her life, but greatly enriched it. It is also a call to faith that when we are asked to give what we have, we do so believing that God will multiply that offering. It is a resounding "No" to the message of self-doubt and inadequacy.

At the heart of the story of Esther is an issue that is applicable to men as well as women. It is the question of what every human being was born to be and to do. In chapter 4 of that exciting melodrama, Queen Esther, who had learned of the planned annihilation of her people, the Jews, had received an urgent message from her cousin Mordecai pleading with her to go to the king, to intercede with the king on behalf of her people.

Esther was severely torn and in great jeopardy. Even a queen was not to go before the king unless bidden, and the penalty for an uninvited appearance could be death. Esther reminded Cousin Mordecai of all this in her note back to him, but he insisted, saying: "Who knows whether you have been born into the kingdom for such a time as this?"

Esther's answer was swift and to the point. She asked Mordecai to gather all the Jews and have them fast and pray for three days. She and her maidens would do likewise. At the end of this spiritual preparation, she would go to the king, whatever the risk. "And free me from my fear," she prayed. This was both a cry of anguish and a life choice, choosing to let go of the external roles that had defined her previously, and then owning her full power as a woman.

As we know from the story, Esther's bold and courageous schemes, carried out in the midst of tremendous odds, thwarts the impending genocide of her people. Esther does not wait for permission from the authorities, but approaches the throne of the King with one foot in her culture and one foot in God's eternal now, where new possibilities abound. Though God is never mentioned in this celebrated story, it was, indeed, God's plan that Esther would be in the kingdom "for such a time as this."

What was true of Esther's story is true of us. Whatever we have and are is part of a calling. Our talents are to be risked in the places to which we are assigned. The stories in the survey constitute a collective story of women who like Esther did not wait for permission from the authorities, from the powers that be. Instead, they too took events into their own hands to become catalysts for change, and thus to secure a new hope-filled future, refusing to be relegated to a prescribed fate and a prescribed role in the life of the church. We are all in this kingdom, in this Mennonite denomination, for this time; and there is no better way to live than in the will of God for our lives.

And finally, I am intrigued by the strange and compelling ending in the Gospel of Mark. Mark concludes, not with shouts of joy and praise, not with the disciples gathered in wonder, amazement, and exultation, but with three women fleeing the empty tomb. "Go Tell," the angel said. And they go all right, running down the road, away from the garden, with terror choking their throats. But they don't tell! Why would they tell nothing to anyone?

The narrator's explanation is a climactic two-word sentence in Greek, translated in English which means . . . "for they were afraid." We can sympathize with that fear. There is the fear of persecution for being identified with a crucified man. There is the potential of mockery since women were considered unreliable witnesses. Could something said by women be considered believable? The response of others to their witness might be like the old priest Eli, who watched Hannah from his seat outside the temple. He observed her silent prayer in which only her lips move; it seemed to him so unusual that he took her to be drunk.

The effect of Mark's ending opens up a whole new plot, for a whole new mystery is introduced. The story leaves the listener with a major puzzle: will the story be told? To whatever degree we as listeners can identify with the women's fear, the question about whether the story will be told is a question we must ask ourselves. The story requires each of us to reflect on the response of running away from this commission and remaining silent. It is up to each of us to decide how the story will end.

But, you know, the final ending of Mark's gospel comes not when the women begin running down the road but a few verses before that when the angel says to them: "Go, tell his disciples and Peter that Jesus is going before you to Galilee; there you will see him, as he told you." Jesus did not rise from the dead and disappear. Jesus did not leave the women alone as they tried to find the courage to tell the story. Jesus rose to meet them and us in Galilee.

The women fled the empty tomb's amazing and terrifying promise of a new life and a new world. They thought they were returning to the old familiar life they knew and understood. But it was already gone. Christ was already in Galilee. Each of us must decide what Galilee means for us as that place of new possibility and new potential. Christ is already there, calling us to meet him. Christ is already in the church, breaking down the walls between male and female, equipping both women and men to serve in his name and be disciples of the good news. In the midst of our fearfulness, Christ greets us in a fresh and reshaped world of life and love.

Kierkegaard talks somewhere about the "alarming possibility of being able." Whether we see our response mirrored in the laughter and doubt of

Sarah, the step of faithfulness into the unknown like the widow of Zarephath, the hesitation of Esther, or the fear of the women at the tomb – in all these we have heard God's yes to us.

So now we can voice to God the "no" of our ambivalence, the "no" of our doubts, the "no" of our hesitations and fears, the "no" of our namelessness. The conflicting messages between call and ambivalence are over. A new conversation has begun with a God who eagerly welcomes and chooses our company. A new conversation has begun, where women's voices are not tentative, frail, or halting; they are growing in strength and confidence. A new conversation has begun that will enable the church to be transformed into a new and living community of women and men sharing ministries equally, valuing relatedness and independence, playing a prophetic role in a world that so desperately needs a new vision.

Our ministry together as women and men is rooted in the future, in new possibilities, and in the faith and inner call experienced so profoundly that "neither life nor death, neither powers nor principalities, neither the present nor the future, neither things in heaven above, nor the earth beneath" . . . nor cultural images of men and women, nor Scripture, nor tradition will keep us from the love of God that is in Christ Jesus, our Lord, who calls us and gives us the work of ministry to do. Amen.

Chapter Five

Some Reflections on Pastoral Ministry and Pastoral Education

Marlin E. Miller

The following was presented on November 3, 1991, to the annual Directors' meeting of the Conference Based Theological Education, an extension program related to Eastern Mennonite Seminary of Harrisonburg, Virginia, and Associated Mennonite Biblical Seminary of Elkhart, Indiana.

I need to start with a confession. Because of time constraints, I shall plagiarize parts of a presentation I made last January during Associated Mennonite Biblical Seminary Pastors' Week. Moreover, I would like to approach this presentation differently than I had originally intended and begin with some introductory remarks that are somewhat autobiographical. This part will be extemporaneous. It will either be the work of the Spirit or the foolishness of a human being! I shall then move to several points that I summarized last January in relation to the Pauline theology and understanding of pastoral ministry. Finally, I would like to close with three emphases for pastoral education.

I. An Autobiographical Introduction

I came to Goshen Biblical Seminary as a student in 1960-61. That preceded what later came to be called the "Dean's Seminar," a sort of foundational exercise for Mennonite Biblical Seminary and Goshen Biblical Seminary faculty to develop a new vision of theological education. I remained at Goshen Biblical Seminary (and on occasional days at Mennonite Biblical Seminary) for only one year, but over the years I kept in touch with developments at the seminaries. At the time that I came as a student, several faculty members criticized "pastoral ministry" and "pastoral office" on the basis of what was presumed to be a more biblical and a more radically Anabaptist vision of the "priesthood of all believers."

The memories that I have from those days and of what came out of the Dean's Seminar were that Anabaptists stood for the "priesthood of all believers." Protestants stood for a kind of pastoral ministry that undermined the priesthood of all believers and localized Christian ministry in the office of the pastor. In order to move away from the unfinished Protestant Reformation, we needed to recover the Anabaptist vision of the priesthood of all believers. We needed to recover the Pauline theology that teaches that the gifts of the Holy Spirit are given to everyone. We needed to develop a completely new understanding of ministry and to work out a completely new understanding of theological education. This understanding would not focus on pastoral ministry, but on an education for everyone to exercise their ministry in the congregation. Ministry would then depend upon the particular callings of particular people in particular contexts. It would not include some notion of a pattern of pastoral ministry or of an office of pastoral ministry that would be more or less constant in a variety of congregational settings.

That summarizes very rapidly an orientation that has been part of the legacy of Associated Mennonite Biblical Seminary and that has been for better or for worse, or for a combination of the two, something of the orientation in relation to the theology of pastoral ministry that has been nurtured here.

After a year at Goshen Biblical Seminary in 1960-61, I continued my study in two European settings. After completing graduate work, I ended up as part of a pastoral team in a small congregation in the suburbs of Paris, France. In the course of that period of time, about six years, I began to wonder more existentially and experientially about the notion of the priesthood of all believers interpreted in a way that seemed to undermine the specific characteristics of pastoral ministry. In the Paris congregation and in many other congregations among French Mennonites and among some Protestant churches, and to some degree in Roman Catholic parishes, it seemed to me that very much depended upon the quality of congregational leadership. The notion that if everyone got together and exercised their particular gift and the Holy Spirit would automatically make things comes out correctly became less credible. Simultaneously, it seemed like calling the "priesthood of all believers" into question would mean going against the Anabaptists and the Apostle Paul. They were rather formidable opponents!

After several years we returned to Elkhart County for a year's furlough. Instead of returning to Paris as planned, we remained here. And I began to work on matters of theological education and pastoral ministry from still other perspectives in the seminary setting.

In the last few years, and partially by request, I have needed to work further with notions about pastoral ministry and the priesthood of all believers. I discovered that some of the scholarship on which I was basing my earlier opinions was not well founded, that it was at least distorted. A couple of years ago C. J. Dyck asked me to write an article on the "priesthood of all believers" for the new volume of the Mennonite Encyclopedia. So I went back through many of the Anabaptist sources looking for the understanding of the priesthood of all believers that I had heard about in the '60s and had read about from several Mennonite and other-than-Mennonite authors as being attributed to the Radical Reformation. I found only two pages in any of the Anabaptist and Mennonite sources in the sixteenth century explicitly on the "priesthood of all believers." Those two pages were in Menno Simons' Complete Works. They gave a fairly straightforward and simple interpretation of the concept of the priesthood of believers in 1 Peter and Revelation. Menno picked up on those passages and talked about Christians being a royal priesthood in terms of living a holy life and in terms of witnessing to the world. There was no whisper of anything in the priesthood of all believers having to do directly with a particular theology of ministry. There was nothing in Menno that would argue against the legitimacy of pastoral ministry as a specific ministry and as a specific gift in the church because of the priesthood of all believers.

Since I had not specialized in Anabaptist studies but had only made a hobby out of it, I assumed that I was probably overlooking something. After all, the people I had been reading were scholars of the sixteenth-century Anabaptist movement! So I checked with C. J. Dyck and asked whether he knew of anything I was missing. He couldn't think of anything else, and said my findings were probably correct. He had, in fact, suspected as much but had never checked it out. Rightly or wrongly, I thought that C. J. must know and so went on from there.

One place that I found something about the "priesthood of all believers" in the century was in Martin Luther's writings. And he interpreted it to say (among other things) that because everyone is a priest, and if the Pope and the clergy didn't reform the church, that the princes who had power in society could use their position to reform the church. That wasn't what Mennonites would tend to say! It hasn't occurred to most Mennonites so far to ask a Brian Mulroney or a George Bush to reform the church! But that is in nontechnical terms one sense in which Martin Luther was using the concept.

Then I began to wonder if recent Anabaptist scholarship had been trying to say that we are all called to be Christian ministers, and that in order to say that, had used the concept of the priesthood of all believers in ways that claimed to be from the Anabaptist movement but historically were not there. I further wondered whether something similar was going on with our understanding of Paul. Does Paul's theology of gifts eliminate the legitimacy of pastoral ministry as a particular calling, as a particular ministry, in the midst of other Christian ministries? That brings me to some of the background questions I had coming to the assignment that was given to me for Pastors' Week last January, to summarize the Pauline understandings of ministry.

To wrap up the autobiographical side, I would say that over a period of years, partly through a re-examination of both the theological and the exegetical sides of the question, and partly through needing to face the issues in terms of serving as a pastor and as a seminary educator, I have come out somewhat differently than where I was in 1960. Hopefully, that is a constructive sign! I would also solicit your perspective and your advice and counsel on these matters. I have come to the conclusion that pastoral ministry has been among the more controversial and significant debates and points of uncertainty among us in the last thirty years. I am concerned about how we can respond most faithfully in the coming years.

II. Pastoral Ministry in the Pauline Writings

Let us move now to some of the major points in the Pauline understanding of Christian ministry. I shall not try to summarize the biblical understanding of Christian ministry, but limit my remarks on the Pauline understanding. It is from interpretations of Paul's understanding of ministry that have most frequently come the sort of foundational criticisms that supposedly undermine the legitimacy of pastoral office or pastoral ministry.

First, on the place of Christian ministry within Paul's perspective: we need to remind ourselves that in Paul's perspective, the place of Christian ministry is within the community of believers, within the church, within the people of the future who are living in the present. The diverse ministries (and there are many diverse ministries mentioned in the Pauline epistles) are all ministries of the church and in the church rather than being identified with jobs or activities in the broader society. Paul does not characterize his tent making as ministry. He does encourage Christians to work, says that work has dignity, that it is a means of caring for others, that it is a means of caring for one's family, and that it is a means of sharing resources with other believers. But he doesn't describe "work" as "ministry."

He does not describe "professions" that we exercise in the broader society as Christian ministry. Through Lutheran influences and through contemporary Mennonite efforts to enhance the relevance of what we as Christians do in the broader society, we have tended frequently to adopt the notion that what we do in our jobs is ministry. I think it is commendable to see what we do in the broader society as an expression of Christian discipleship. But there is in the New Testament perspective, particularly within the Pauline perspective and more broadly, a distinction between church and world, between the believing community and the surrounding world. And ministry is a concept that is particularly related to those things that are carried out within the church and in the church's mission in the broader world.

A second observation: in the Pauline epistles the source of Christian ministries is attributed variously to the Holy Spirit or to the exalted Lord at work in the church during the interim time between the resurrection of Christ and the return of Christ. Because the Spirit or the exalted Lord is the source of ministry, the normal situation of the church is one in which there is a rich variety and a great diversity of ministries and gifts given to the church for the common good. That much of the view and interpretation that I reported as a part of my own journey, I think, is a correct interpretation of the Pauline view of ministry. Paul encourages Christians to see that there are more rather than fewer ministries. But it seems to me that some in Mennonite circles have tended to push that view too far by insisting that everyone has an identifiable ministry, to make out of that thesis a kind of moral obligation, and further, to use that thesis as a way of undermining the distinctive calling of pastoral ministry.

I think the exegetical basis for this view is overdone or perhaps even nonexistent. More specifically, the exegetical basis for the combined notion that everyone has a ministry and that there are no significant differences between other ministries and pastoral ministry is based ostensibly on Romans 12:3, 1 Corinthians 7:7, and Ephesians 4:7. You find this interpretation especially in the writings of John Yoder. Those passages speak about everyone having a gift. But if you look a little more closely at the Pauline language, he uses a different kind of language to underscore "each and everyone" than he uses in these particular passages. In 1 Thessalonians 2:11 and 2 Thessalonians 1:3, for example, he uses "*heis hekastos*" to emphasize "each and every one." He does not use this phrase in Romans 12:3; he does not use it in 1 Corinthians 7:7. He uses another term that is more general and less insistent on "all" in the sense of "each and every one." Thus there is a nuanced difference in the language of the Pauline epistles. In Ephesians 4:7 the more specialized "each and every one" is used in the reference to "grace," but not directly for the specific ministries of verses 11ff. It seems to me that we should affirm, on the basis of the Pauline writings, that because the Spirit or the exalted Lord is the source of ministry, the normal situation in the church is a rich diversity and variety of ministries. But if we press that view in the direction of making a law out of "each and every one" having an identifiable ministry in the same sense as a pastoral ministry or a teaching ministry or an evangelistic ministry, we are going beyond the exegetical basis and overinterpreting the text.

A third point: what is pastoral ministry in a narrower sense against the backdrop of the diversity of ministries referred to in the Pauline epistles? Here I would like to make five points that I believe are the major points in the Pauline writings with regard to what we may call "pastoral ministry."

1. First, there are several terms that are used in the Pauline writings that seem to be synonymous. I would refer you to the document *Leadership and Authority in the Church* that was adopted in the Mennonite Church in 1981 for the details. The terms "overseer," "bishop," and "pastor" seem to be more or less synonymous in the Pauline epistles. And if one looks at all those passages, the terms apparently refer to a group of persons who are responsible for the community oversight, care, and leadership. Oversight, care, and leadership of the community as a whole would be the point of these different terms. Now why these different terms are used is not absolutely clear. It seems that they come from the different cultural contexts of the early Christians, with "elder" coming out of the synagogue context, and "bishop" and "overseer" being related more to the Roman or Hellenistic contexts. Essentially they tend to be synonymous in their point of reference. That means, however, that the use that churches have frequently made of those terms in church history or in the history of theology is rather different from the way they are used in Scripture.

2. Secondly, the "elders" responsible for community oversight are frequently linked with what is called "teaching," particularly Ephesians 4:11, 1 Timothy 5:17, and perhaps Romans 12:7. Perhaps it is implicit in Romans 12:7 that teaching is a part of this ministry. In any case, teaching is an important part of eldering and, apparently, judging from the Timothy reference, the overseers or bishops or pastors or elders could also frequently serve as teachers.

Teaching had to do with both transmitting the tradition and with addressing contemporary challenges. It focused on what we might call the normative beliefs and practices of the faith community. Scattered throughout the Pauline epistles, the apostle refers to the way we "teach in all the churches" or argues against people who are trying to deviate from normative convictions or develops some perspectives that others may not yet have understood. These efforts are always aimed at what should count as normative beliefs and practices, not just Paul's own opinions. When he is talking about his own opinions, he says so. But the teachers, the elders, are people who are to care particularly for the normative beliefs and practices of the faith community.

3. A third thing that relates to "pastoral ministry" (although not exclusively) is equipping others for ministry. The term "equip" is a direct quotation from Ephesians 4, and is not limited to the overseer-bishop-elder ministry. It probably also belongs to the prophetic and apostolic ministries. But the equipping of others seems to be a part of these particular ministries for the apostle Paul. Extrapolating from this observation, exercising these ministries should not discourage other ministries in the church, but encourage them, nurture them, call them forth, mentor them. It seems to me that this aspect is very important because we have sometimes gotten into the bind of thinking that if we call particular people to particular ministries, we more or less automatically discourage others from exercising their ministries. In the Pauline vision, people are called to a pastoral ministry to encourage others, to mentor others, and to build up others, not to exclude them from Christian ministries.

4. A fourth thing that comes out in these Pauline writings is that at least sometimes elders, and particularly teaching elders, are given financial support to provide the time that would otherwise be needed to earn a living. This is not necessarily a universal rule. We know well enough that the apostle Paul did not claim this kind of privilege. That had to do with his understanding of his particular mission and of his strategy of mission that really financial support would be justified, but unwise, under those circumstances. Thus there is biblical precedent for providing financial support for people engaged in these types of ministries, even though it may also be better under some conditions to find other means of support.

5. Finally, the qualifications for an elder-bishop-overseer-pastor are phrased primarily in terms of attitudes, integrity between public and private life, conduct, and familiarity with Scriptures and traditions. This series of things may be lumped together in the term qualifications that have to do with

the minister's "character." One's character is exemplified in the way one lives, in the way one conducts oneself in the family, in the way one conducts oneself with people outside the faith community. I have been involved in some conference debates in which "husbands of one wife" (1 Timothy 3:2) is interpreted to mean that women may not be "bishops" or pastors. That seems to me a little beside the main point. The point of the series in 1 Timothy 3 is to identify the quality of character, the fidelity of persons that is demonstrated by being monogamous rather than polygamous. Most other items in 1 Timothy 3 can also be generalized in terms of quality of character.

I really doubt that we can go much further than these five points in summarizing what the ministry of overseer-bishop-elder-pastor means in the Pauline epistles. Most other interpretations that we give to this ministry need to be considered theological extrapolations that may well be legitimate. But we should not over read what we find in the texts; and I don't think we find much more in the texts. If others of you have found more key characteristics of pastoral ministry, I would appreciate your sharing them.

III. Priorities for Pastoral Ministry

Based on these five observations of this particular ministry in the midst of many other ministries in the New Testament, I would like to make five suggestions on what might be the highest priorities of pastoral ministry. Here I am also introducing new terminology and speaking about a particular "role" or "office" in our context. "Office," of course, is not a biblical term. By this term, however, I mean a pattern of expectations about understandings and practices of ministry that fit together in a congruent way.

1. First of all, I suggest that a major aspect of pastoral ministry be based on the Pauline vision of congregational oversight in the sense of providing guidance for the welfare of the congregation as a whole. This particular ministry of bishop-overseer-pastor is oriented toward the whole group, not only toward specific persons or specific parts of the group. It relates to the whole, tries to get a vision of the whole, tries to be concerned with the overall work of the church. This calls at least partially into question some of the emphases that have developed in our time and context on pastoral ministry. Some of these emphases have gone rather far in terms of focusing pastoral ministry on one-to-one care.

And at times in the past twenty to thirty years, seminaries have put a lot of emphasis on pastoral counseling in the sense of one-on-one care that can almost consume an entire week. When that happens, pastors lose out in terms of the vision of the church as a whole, of the congregation as a whole, of the group of believers as a whole. What this aspect means practically needs to be worked out. It doesn't mean that pastors should be unconcerned about the care of individuals. But it seems to me that addressing the care of the whole group, particularly through corporate decision making, through corporate worship, through corporate "administration," are major concerns; other things will then also need to find their proper place as well.

2. The second major aspect of the pastoral role is teaching, providing leadership in discerning, and passing on normative Christian beliefs and practices. This would include normative beliefs and practices in worship, piety, and ethics. What are the core beliefs; what are the core practices that really capture who we are as a faith community and that provide continuity for it? We live in a very pluralistic society, in a post enlightenment democratic society. Mennonites have tended frequently to be a little suspicious of normative beliefs and practices. We have even misused them and sometimes forced them down people's throats, so to speak. But unless we are able to develop, pass on, and articulate normative beliefs and practices, we are not really following out the teaching dimension of pastoral ministry, and, I think, we will be in serious trouble as faith communities.

George Lindbeck, Professor of Historical Theology at Yale Divinity School, has made a big point about the disintegration of Christian identity in American Protestantism. He feels that one of the basic problems is the loss of normative beliefs and practices. Based on a New Testament emphasis on the role of teaching, it seems we need to recapture something of a vision for teaching as a particular responsibility of pastoral ministry in order to cultivate and nurture Christian (and Mennonite) identity in our pluralistic society.

3. A third aspect would be the nurturing and empowering of other members – ministries through mentoring and training. I know very few congregations that have written nurturing and mentoring others in their ministry into the pastoral job description. Practically, one person cannot do a lot of mentoring. But at least, it seems to me, if every pastor were mentoring and nurturing two or three other people every two or three years, developing others' gifts could be an important responsibility of pastoral ministry. Paul mentored Timothy and others as part of his apostolic and teaching ministry.

4. A fourth aspect is what we would normally call pastoral care and leadership in the faith community, walking with and helping others walk with members during crises or life transitions. Although that doesn't all need to be

done by a pastor, general oversight in this area certainly would be a part of pastoral ministry.

5. A fifth aspect is something that can be extrapolated from the apparent plurality of such pastors in a local congregation. There has been a lot of discussion in recent years that the pastor or the pastors should work together with others in the congregation who are "co-ministers." We see in the Pauline writings and in many of the Mennonite traditions (with different terms) an understanding of pastoral ministry that is exercised by several people in a congregation. One or more of them may be full time; others may be less than full time. Some of our current patterns undermine this tradition in the sense that we may have "elders" who are elected for two or three years. When that happens, there isn't much continuity; they can't be a part of a team that provides longer-term support for a full-time pastor; and they can't provide the kind of eldering which demands continuity, shared vision, and longer-term service.

IV. Implications for Pastoral Education

Finally, what are some implications for pastoral education? I would like to refer to three areas in general without developing them extensively. Perhaps the responses or discussion can push these issues out a bit more.

1. First, I suggest that an important part of pastoral education would be what may be called "character formation." I'm consciously not using the term "spiritual formation" (although we're using it at AMBS presently) because it seems to me that we need to look at this area a bit more broadly than only spiritual formation understood in the narrower sense of encouraging the disciplines of prayer, Scripture, meditation, spiritual retreats, and the like. Those are all fine and wonderful and necessary, and there are many reasons they should be nurtured as a means of maintaining and strengthening one's relationship to God. But by "character" I mean something that includes the individual's relationship to God but also extends to interpersonal relations and to how we live within the faith community and in the larger society. The "formation" of "character" underscores the importance of community as well as the formation of my personal relationship with God.

It seems to me that we are in danger of taking a somewhat more individualistic approach if we buy uncritically into some of the things that are considered spiritual formation. In order to provide needed correctives, it may help to emphasize "character formation." To interpret and extrapolate from the passages in the Pauline epistles, to which I referred earlier, character was formed through the way one lived in the family, through the way one lived in the broader community, and through the expressions of life in these faith and other communities. Thus, what counts is not only praying a lot (although praying a lot is good); what counts is not only that we read the Scriptures a lot (although that is also very good); but what also counts is how we are formed by interacting with other people, by responsibility in family and in society.

I was struck several years ago while talking with Marcus Smucker, who directs the Spiritual Formation program here, with his comments on the "delayed adolescence" of many American young people. The period of adolescence has moved in many ways from the mid-teens to mid-twenties (or even later). We were speculating why that is so. Marcus suggested that part of the reason may be postponement of vocational decisions, of whether to remain single or to marry, of delaying children if one is married. A whole series of such things shape character by a participation in a broader community or in a broader social unit. Delaying these character-shaping events may also delay maturation. That's something of what I mean when speaking about character formation.

It seems to me that in pastoral education we need to give attention to character formation, a part of which includes what we are now calling spiritual formation, with some kind of corporate discipline, corporate responsibility, and corporate worship as well as the individual discipline, individual responsibility, and individual worship. Such an approach might well reinforce (or make plausible) an understanding of pastoral ministry as that ministry which gives particular attention to the congregation as a whole.

2. A second major component of pastoral education would be helping people who are to assume pastoral ministry develop clear understandings, acceptance, and interpretation of what we can call normative Christian beliefs and practices. What is "orthodoxy" and what is "orthopraxis," to use some of the contemporary terminology that is thrown around? I'm impressed by the fact that in the Protestant theological enterprise there is currently much discussion about the nature of theological education. One of the minority voices has come recently out of Andover-Newton Seminary in a book by Max Stackhouse called *Apologia* (apologetics). He is arguing that liberal Protestant seminaries need to find their way back to "defending" core Christian beliefs in the midst of our pluralistic age. To be sure, he only has four such core beliefs: sin and salvation, biblical revelation, trinity, and Christology. Nevertheless, these are some fairly foundational beliefs.

As Anabaptists and Mennonites, we would doubtless want to add some "core practices." It seems to me, in talking with students, seminary faculty members, and pastors these days, that as Mennonites engaged in pastoral education, we need to risk "promoting" normative beliefs and practices. We can't depend upon ethnic continuities without corporate conversation and discipline to nurture Mennonite identity. We should also spell out the importance of normative beliefs and practices in terms of biblical studies, historical studies, theological studies, and ethical studies in order to keep this agenda central in pastoral education.

3. Third, in addition to character formation and to nurturing normative beliefs and practices, pastoral education should include what we might call the "arts" of pastoral ministry. Some talk about "skills" or "competencies." That's fine, as long as those terms aren't taken too mechanically. I would prefer to use a term like the "arts" of pastoral ministry. I would suggest, at least for our discussion, four or five areas where the ministerial arts are critical for pastoral ministry and should, therefore, be emphasized in pastoral education.

One is good communication, whether publicly in preaching and teaching, or in more personal settings. The major tools of pastors are words. If we can't use words helpfully and constructively, we might as well hang up our shovel and hoe. Communication, of course, includes many things besides words. But if you stumble around as a pastor and say things like "Well, you know what I mean," most people won't. Communication is very crucial.

A second area of ministerial arts may be termed "representative events" of the faith community: worship, baptism, communion, funerals, and the like. Pastors, with the help of others, have a key role to play in focusing the life and practice of a community in and during these representative events. These representative events are very important. They nurture the life of the community; they address the community as a whole; they communicate something of what the church is about to the broader society. The representational quality of these events is very important. The exercise of those ministerial arts is related to them and is also crucial.

Seminaries and other pastoral training programs generally work on these first two arts of ministry. A third one has not been developed very consciously in pastoral education. We haven't even lifted it up high enough to know whether we are succeeding or failing at it. I'm referring to the art of mentoring others in their ministries. Including the mentoring of others in their ministries as a key ministerial art would seem to be very important if we are trying to follow the Pauline vision and the Anabaptist vision of pastoral ministry. But we still need to work out what that may mean concretely for pastoral education.

A fourth area of pastoral education would be collaboration with co-ministers. One of the things that impressed me after having been away from the United States for several years (1961-1974) was learning that many congregations had moved from having several ministers (at least in the "Old" Mennonite tradition) to having one pastor. I kept asking people as I traveled to several congregations when and why that had happened. It didn't happen only because somebody went off to seminary and got formal training to be a pastor. It frequently happened because there were squabbles between the ministers. One pragmatic way of resolving the squabbles and of bringing peace to the congregation was to eliminate all pastors but one, on the assumption that one pastor could not fight with herself or himself. Since then (likely this was also known earlier!) we have also discovered that it's possible for congregations and pastors to squabble with each other.

I'm not proposing that having one (full-time) pastor in a congregation is wrong nor that having several ministers is always right. What I am suggesting is that if we want to develop pastoral ministry in ways that nurture and call out the gifts of others in the church, one way we might do that is to learn to develop the ministerial arts of collaborating with others who also exercise responsibility in the congregation.

Finally, the fifth major area of pastoral education would be in pastoral care, or as the longer-term Christian tradition would say, "care of souls." Pastoral education will certainly employ the disciplines of counseling, but do so in ways that include nurturing both the individual believer's and the whole community's relationship with God in the context of their life as a whole.

So those are several remarks, partly autobiographical and partly related to ongoing conversations over the years. I would be interested in your responses and perspectives.

Chapter Six

The Mutuality of Ministry:
A Dialogue with Mark

Lydia Neufeld Harder

> Lydia Neufeld Harder wrote this paper after several related oral
> presentations during the academic year of 1993-94, during which
> time she served as an interim faculty member at Canadian
> Mennonite Bible College, Winnipeg, Manitoba.

A dialogue with the Gospel of Mark about the nature of ministry
begins by listening carefully to the way that Mark tells the story of Jesus and
his disciples. The narrative form of the Gospel implies that Mark's theology
will not be presented in logical, conceptual form. Instead, readers are invited
to identify with the various characters in the story. They are challenged to
discern the meaning of the events by an active engagement with the questions
that are raised as the plot shifts and as conflicts escalate. Dialogue about
ministry cannot, therefore, wait until a theology is abstracted from the story.
Rather, reflective reading begins by noting the different ways in which the
Gospel writer and the reader evaluate specific events and persons in the story.
Questions that open us to Mark's theology surface when similar or differing
assumptions are identified. The very act of reading thus implies an exploration
of the tensions and ambiguities that arise within us when the horizons of past
and present meet in the reading process.[1]

This essay will begin by reflecting on the way that we as ministering
persons, standing in a Mennonite faith tradition, tend to identify with the
narrative. It will recognize that most of us who stand within a Christian
tradition are re-readers of the story and already have fixed patterns of
identification that can help or hinder us from hearing the message that Mark
wants to give us. The essay will therefore invite us to re-think this
identification in line with the direction that Mark gives to us through his

---

[1] This approach resembles reader-response criticism because it consciously examines
the way we as readers tend to determine the meaning of the Gospel. My reading
assumes a reader who wishes to know the will of God as revealed through the reading
of the Bible. For an exploration of the method see: Janice Capel Anderson and
Stephen D. Moore, eds., *Mark and Method (Augsburg, 1992), chap. 3.*

telling of the story. In this way we hope to discover a theology of ministry that empowers us to serve effectively and with integrity in the name of Jesus, the Christ.

I. Naming the Traditions of Ministry

When Mennonites look for a paradigm of ministry within the Gospel narrative, they tend to turn very quickly to Jesus as a primary model of ministry and service. Though this presents us with an ideal to strive for, it also diverts us from identifying with the disciples and their entry into ministry. It allows us to focus on a perfectionist vision of what disciples should be rather than a realistic vision of what disciples can become. It introduces a norm against which we can measure ourselves but sometimes fails to give us an identity that can empower us. It may even encourage a false association with divine authority rather than noting our need for dependence on God's grace and empowerment. An immediate identification with Jesus may thus discourage us from exposing our hidden selves to God's redemptive and healing action. The mutuality that is inherent in a ministry that both receives and gives may be concealed from our eyes.

Elizabeth Struthers Malbon proposes an alternative modeling that is present in the Gospel stories. She points to the followers of Jesus who are portrayed in the Gospel of Mark "with both strong points and weak points in order to serve as realistic and encouraging models for hearers/readers who experience both strength and weakness in their Christian discipleship."[2] This approach suggests that though we may look to Jesus' words and actions for an evaluative framework for ministry in the church, we must look to the narratives of discipleship for realistic paradigms of ministry.

As we turn to the Gospel of Mark, we probably remember rather easily the particular disciple group who is explicitly called to the work of ministry – to "fish for people" (1:17), to "proclaim the message, and to have authority to cast out demons" (3:14-15). That story of blessing, temptation, and opportunity is told in some detail, thus leading many of us to identify closely with this official ministering group of followers. However, the twelve disciples are not the only group of followers whose story is told in the gospel of Mark. Another disciple group is entrusted with the message that Jesus has been raised and is told to "go, tell his disciples and Peter that he is going

---

[2]Elizabeth Struthers Malbon, "Disciples/Crowds/Whoever: Markan Characters and Readers," *Novum Testamentum XXVIII, No.2* (1986), p. 104.

ahead of you into Galilee" (16:7). This less official story also elicits certain identifications – identifications that have become particularly important to women.

These stories of Jesus' followers provide two distinct paradigms describing two ways of entering ministry and service in the community of disciples. What strikes us initially as we compare the description of these two groups of disciples is the way that gender seems to determine who is named and recognized in the story. The twelve men are officially called to the ministry of Jesus on a mountain, a symbolic reminder of another mountain with key importance for the covenant people. Their story becomes public knowledge and receives public recognition in the oral and written traditions of the early Christian church.

In contrast, the women's stories are hidden in the story of the crowd of people around Jesus. Their story almost becomes a postscript on discipleship, a story recounted only very briefly in the public record (15:41). Feminist biblical scholars are beginning to insist that female stories must be named as traditions of ministry even though their story is told with less detail than the male story. They suggest that the marginalization of certain stories of discipleship and the prominence of others need not necessarily imply that God also evaluates the ministry of women as secondary and less important.[3]

If we begin by accepting both traditions as traditions of ministry, we must ask why the women's story is told with less detail than the male story. Does the marginalization of certain stories of discipleship and the prominence of others necessarily imply that God also evaluates the ministry of women as secondary and less important? A number of scholars are suggesting that this way of telling the story fits into the androcentric (male-centered) cultural milieu of the times where men were usually the writers and the heroes of public literature. They are acknowledging that the androcentricism of the biblical text witnesses to the human mediation of God's word and to the historical particularity of the biblical text.

However, this raises a second key question for us. What is the significance of the sudden appearance of female followers in 15:40-41? Why do these disciples become so prominent in the climactic ending of the story?

---

[3]Winsome Munro, "Women Disciples in Mark?" *Catholic Biblical Quarterly 44* (1982), pp. 225-241; Elizabeth Schussler Fiorenza, *In Memory of Her* (New York: Crossroad, 1984), pp. 316-323.

Why does their ministry suddenly become acknowledged in the official story? What is meant by this breaking of a cultural pattern?

In a more careful study of the way the followers of Jesus are named Mark demonstrates that the term disciple includes others beyond the circle of the Twelve. This inclusiveness is clearly indicated when Jesus asserts that those who are his kin, his "mother, brother, and sister," are those who do the will of God (3:31-35). Elizabeth Schussler Fiorenza has pointed out that Mark's use of three verbs to characterize the women's discipleship points to their inclusion not only as disciples but as true apostolic witnesses. The women followed (*akolouthein*), ministered or served (*diakonein*), and came up with Jesus to Jerusalem (*synanabainein*).[4]

These verbs remind of us of the call and decision to follow, the mandate to serve, and the challenge to go with Jesus to the cross, key experiences which also validate the male disciples as witnesses and proclaimers of the Jesus event. They remind us that though cultural patterns have often determined who can be official ministers, it was not these patterns which brought women into the official story of ministry. Rather, it was God's direct call to the women that subverted and challenged limited notions of who could be effective witnesses for God. The ending of Mark clearly indicates a new direction for ministry, a direction which includes both women and men in the official naming of ministers.[5]

The differences between the two traditions of ministry point not only to the difference between male and female ministry as described in Mark. They also point to a difference in the way disciples of Jesus throughout the ages have experienced their role in the ministry of the church. Some disciples have been publicly recognized as ministers in the church; others have served quietly behind the scenes. The fact that this difference in official recognition has often coincided with gender or class differentiation suggests that we should reconsider how official and unofficial ministry relate to each other.

---

[4]Fiorenza, *In Memory of Her*, pp. 320-321.

[5]Throughout this essay I am concurring with many scholars who would assume that verse 8 is the original ending of the Gospel of Mark. Note the endings in both the NIV and the NRSV. A number of scholars suggest that the abrupt ending asks the reader to respond in line with the challenges presented in the story thus far. See, for example, Mary Ann Tolbert, *Sowing the Gospel* (Minneapolis: Fortress Press, 1989), p. 295ff.

Can mutual respect and dynamic interaction determine these relationships rather than domination or competition between sexes and classes?

Though the Gospel of Mark resembles the culture of the time in the way it describes male and female ministry, it also begins a process of subversion of this evaluation by pointing to a new direction for the relationship between official and unofficial ministry. This process is detected if we look more closely at how the narrative describes the temptations and challenges of each of the disciple groups.

If we can acknowledge that gender differences are not the most important differences between the two paradigms of discipleship, both women and men are free to identify with either of these traditions. Throughout history some disciples, both male and female, have been publicly recognized as ministers in the church. Others, both male and female, have served quietly behind the scenes. As we follow the narrative identifying with each tradition in turn, we will be able to note the difference in experience that official recognition makes. We will be able to reflect on the unique temptations and challenges that often accompany official ministry as well as unofficial ministry. We will be able to see how Mark's narrative challenges readers to bring these intertwining traditions together and to supply an ending to the narrative that will allow ministry to continue so that the good news will be proclaimed.

II. The Ministry of the Twelve (the official ministry)

In the Gospel of Mark the ministry of the Twelve begins almost at the same time as the ministry of Jesus. Peter, James, and John are already called to follow in chapter 1 and by chapter 3 the Twelve are appointed as apostles, sent out to proclaim the message of Jesus, and given authority to cast out demons (3:13-19). At the same time, the Twelve are described as insiders who are given special explanations of the parables (4:10-11). In chapter 6 their ministry is again affirmed as they are given a particular assignment and a special empowerment. The Twelve are thus pictured as active participants in the healing and teaching ministry, persons commissioned by Jesus and publicly recognized as leaders in the Jesus movement.

As the narrative unfolds, we note how quickly Jesus' ministry, and therefore the disciples' ministry, becomes controversial. The Twelve very soon become aware that authority conflicts arise when divine power is mediated through an unauthorized person and in an unauthorized way (2:1-16). They soon discover that even a ministry of healing challenges the status quo and enrages the established leaders of the people (3:1-6). As followers of Jesus, the Twelve become involved in symbolic actions such as plucking grain on the Sabbath (chap. 3). At times they support Jesus' interpretations of the Scriptures by not observing the ceremonial washings (chap. 7). They thus participate with Jesus in confronting several of the accepted norms of the community. They discover that with their special assignment comes the challenge to state their central loyalties, to discern the direction of God's actions, and to make judgments about the nature of the mission of Jesus (8:27-30).

After such a strong beginning, it is striking that the Twelve do not continue to be described as ideal models or heroes. Commentators have puzzled over the meaning of a description of leadership that is brutally honest about inadequacy and failure. Was this a polemic against the authority of the Twelve in the early church? Or is this description an honest look at the real temptations and challenges that the Twelve faced as they followed Jesus?

As the narrative continues, we note that nothing characterizes the Twelve more than misunderstanding and fear. Though the disciples had seen many wonders done by Jesus, they trembled in fear as the wind threatened to swamp their boat (4:35-40). Even after seeing the miracle of the feeding of the five thousand, they do not seem to know how to go about feeding the four thousand (8:1-10). Jesus himself reprimands the disciples for not understanding the connection between the two feedings (8:14-21). Though Peter speaks out boldly and confesses Jesus as the Messiah, he misunderstands the nature of that Messiahship and rebukes Jesus when he predicts that his kind of Messiahship leads to suffering and death (8:32-33).

Fear is mentioned three more times in connection with these disciples (9:6; 9:32; 10:32). This fear may be connected to awe and wonder as on the Mount of Transfiguration. But it is also associated with the insecurity of the road that lay ahead of them as they moved toward Jerusalem. However, instead of seeking more understanding, the disciples are afraid to ask Jesus to explain, afraid to face the cost of following (9:31; 10:32). For these disciples, fear seems to indicate a lack of faith and trust in the power and leadership of Jesus.

The response of the Twelve to the fear and insecurity of ministry with Jesus is symbolized by several short incidents in the second half of the Gospel. Here we see the disciples arguing about who is the greatest in the kingdom (9:34) and vying for the places of honor at the time when Jesus will come in his glory (10:37). We find the disciples rebuking those who would bring children to Jesus (10:13) and trying to stop those who were healing in the name of Jesus (9:38). We note how conscious they are that they had left everything to follow Jesus (10:28) and how much they have begun to see themselves not as followers but as those to be followed. James' words symbolize this change when he tries to stop others who were healing and speaks of them as those who are not "following us" (9:39).

This change from following to leading is paralleled by a similar change in the disciples from trust in Jesus to confidence in their own ability. This is particularly demonstrated by Peter, James, and John. They insist on their own ability to withstand temptation. Their self-confidence is almost amusing. James and John respond to the probing questions of Jesus about their ability to drink the cup that Jesus will drink and to be baptized with the baptism that Jesus will be baptized, with an assured "we are able." Peter reacts almost angrily to the prediction of the desertion of the disciples with a confident "even though all become deserters, I will not." Thus, it is not surprising that Peter, James, and John do not pray with Jesus in the garden of Gethsamane. They ignore not only Jesus' request but their own need for empowerment from God. In Mark's narrative, the Twelve all desert Jesus and do not again re-enter the story as ministering people. Hope for their return comes only indirectly in the form of a command to the women in the story to "go, tell his disciples and Peter that you will see him, just as he told you."

Jesus actively tries to teach and admonish his disciples, pointing to a way for them to again become effective ministers. He points to the need for prayer when the disciples cannot heal the boy with a spirit. He points to children and servants as those to whom the kingdom belongs, challenging them to both receive the kingdom as a child and, in turn, to become a servant in their ministry. He challenges them to change their focus from what they have left for the sake of the kingdom to what they are receiving through the kingdom (10:20-30). He warns them of the temptations to lord it over people and to become a tyrant in their leadership role (10:42-45). He invites them to "keep awake and pray that they may not come into the time of trial. . ." (14:38). He even predicts their propensity to fall away when leadership becomes difficult. And finally, when they fail, the message of the young man at the tomb challenges the disciples to listen to the women and to return to Galilee, for "there they will see him, just as he told you."

The story of the temptations and challenges of this official group of ministers ends with failure but also with promise. It ends with a challenge to trust Jesus' words and to receive his empowerment and healing. What is striking is that the promise speaks directly and concretely, suggesting a way to overcome the temptations that have overtaken the disciples thus far in the story. The disciples must receive the message from those often deemed unworthy to publicly proclaim the gospel. They must follow the one who is going ahead of them, for only then will they see him as he is. They will see Jesus in Galilee, the place associated in the Gospel with Jesus' ministry of healing and teaching.[6] Only when they respond in trust, knowing their own brokenness, will they be open to new empowerment that will equip them for ministry in the name of Jesus.

III. The Ministry of the Women (the unofficial ministry)

The ministry of women also begins in Galilee during the early days of Jesus' ministry. We read that "many" women used to follow and serve Jesus there (15:40-41). However, no details are provided, and so we can only imagine that the nature of this service may have been less public. We can assume that this service fitted in well with the cultural norms of the day and so did not warrant an earlier mention in the official story. Women thus represent the unofficial ministry that often does not get public recognition in a community.

Most of the stories of women in the Gospel of Mark fit in with this assumption. They suggest that women serve in the household or through familial relationships. The public contributions of these disciples to the temple or synagogue may have been limited to the giving of alms in support of the public ministry of others. This contribution is, however, highly valued by Jesus as seen in the incident in which he points to the widow, who out of her poverty gave all that she had (12:41-44). The first explicit mention of women's service takes place in a home, a family setting. Here Simon's mother-in-law gets up from her sick bed to serve Jesus and his disciples (1:29). Though not described, we assume that this may have meant preparing a meal or providing clean beds for Jesus and the Twelve on which to sleep.

In several stories women are closely connected to the healing ministry of Jesus. However, they are pictured primarily as recipients rather than as helpers in the healing process. Several stories including that of the

---

[6]Narrative critics have pointed out how Mark's story settings provide an overall framework for the action. The whole story is presented to us as a journey from Galilee to Judea. The geographical settings thus begin to symbolize different parts of Jesus' life. Galilee is thus associated with powerful teaching and healing (chaps. 1-9), while Judea is associated with confrontation and death (chaps. 10-15). See David Rhoads and Donald Michie, *Mark as Story* (Philadelphia: Fortress, 1982), p. 63.

hemorrhaging woman are told of women who were given new life through Jesus' ministering presence. Mary Magdalene, one of the three women mentioned as following Jesus already in Galilee, is identified in the longer ending of Mark as a person from whom Jesus had cast out seven demons (16:9). However, we also have some indication that women were active in bringing others to Jesus. Mark includes the story of people bringing children to Jesus (10:13-16). We can imagine that there were mothers in that group. We also have a specific story in which a mother pleads for the healing of her daughter (7:24-30). Here Jesus is described as explicitly commending her for the words that she speaks. "For saying this, you may go; the demon has left your daughter."

The story of women's ministry that is told with the most detail is the story of the anointing of Jesus for burial in chapter 14. The woman is not named, but her sensitive ministry to Jesus who is facing death is commended. Jesus himself names this personal caring as a good work. "She has performed a good service for me. . . . Wherever the good news is proclaimed in the whole world, what she has done will be told in remembrance of her" (14:9). Jesus publicly defends her ministry since it seems to have become controversial to the people present at the meal. Jesus' answer suggests that personal caring for a friend in need has great value even in the face of the need to give to the poor. This personal service by women followers is again demonstrated in the last story. Here the women gather to go to the tomb to anoint the body of Jesus. This time Jesus is dead and the women are ready to perform the last service to a friend, a service usually assumed by women in the community.

The temptations and challenges of the women who participated in the more unofficial and personal ministry of Jesus have not been recounted in detail. Little indication is given of the choices that these disciples had to make. However, it is clear from the subtle hints given in the story that decisions of faith were also demanded of women. We can assume that it was probably difficult for the widow to choose to give all she had to the temple treasury or for the woman to anoint Jesus in front of disapproving guests. For the women to be present even at a distance at the cross meant taking some risk. Luise Schottroff has pointed out that sometimes the soldiers guarding the cross were given orders to watch for signs of mourning in order to identify followers of the accused.[7] Historically we know that women were also at times crucified.

The fear of the women in face of this threat of persecution is, however, not mentioned. It is not until the women see the young man dressed in a white robe sitting in the tomb that we read of their fear. The young man assures them that they need not be afraid. "Jesus has been raised. Go tell his disciples. . . ." But the Gospel story ends with the women's disobedience to the command of the young man. The women went out from the tomb, "for terror and amazement had seized them; and they said nothing to anyone for they were afraid."

Why were they afraid? Why did they not say anything? Scholars have tried to answer this question in various ways.[8] Some scholars try to excuse the women, assuming that their disobedience was not serious. After all, the Twelve will hear the good news from Jesus directly at a later time. Others speak of the awe that the women felt and minimize the fear. What is clear from other accounts, however, is that the Twelve had a difficult time believing the women when they did overcome their fear and when they attempted to give the disciples the message. The disbelief of these disciples is emphasized three times in the longer endings as well as in the Gospel of Luke (16:11, 13, 14; 24:11). Perhaps the fear experienced by the women is not only related to fear of persecution for themselves. Perhaps the fear is more related to the new responsibility given to them, a responsibility that meant that they had to believe and trust their own experience of God. They had to trust a vision and a commission not authorized by more official authorities. They had to overcome the temptation to flee and to stay hidden in the crowd. Fear thus hindered these women from immediate response to a more public responsibility. For the female disciples, just as for the male disciples, fear was the opposite of trust and faith.

IV. The Movement toward Mutual Ministry

Both the temptations of the Twelve and the temptations of the women at the tomb were connected with fear. The challenges presented to them asked

---

[7]Luise Schottroff, "Maria und die Frauen am Grabe Jesu," *Evangelische Theologie*, 42 (Jan/Feb, 1982), pp. 3-25.

[8]See Fiorenza, p. 322; T. E. Boomershine, "Mark and the Apostolic Commission" *JBL* 100 (1981), pp. 225-39.

both to go beyond the normative expectations that the community had of them – expectations based on gender roles, status, or even official recognition in the community. For the official leaders, the challenge was to give up their need for prestige and their reliance on their own power, and to listen to the message of those who had quietly served in the background. For the unofficial ministers, it meant being willing to go outside of an established role to speak of their own experience of God and to risk rejection and misunderstanding by those whom they may have considered more qualified.

Mark begins the Gospel with the promise of good news. However, for this news to be proclaimed and heard, both groups of followers must overcome their fear and respond to their particular challenge of ministry. Those who had earlier trusted in their own ability had to learn to listen to those who were afraid of the new task entrusted to them. Those who had been afraid to speak overcame their fear and proclaimed the good news to the despairing disciples. This meeting of the traditions of ministry took place in the early church as male and female disciples each overcame fear and responded to the unexpected challenge placed before them. A new trajectory of ministry had begun in which official and unofficial ministers worked side by side in a dynamic relationship of trust and mutuality.

The dialogue with Mark challenges us as well to describe the present reality of ministry in the church honestly and without pretense, naming the differences in status and the need for recognition of the various ministering persons in the community. We are asked to describe the temptations and opportunities that are there within the present social and political realities for those who are officially named and for those who perform ministry more unofficially. We are challenged to be sensitive to God who frequently subverts the human evaluations and classifications of ministry, whether this means affirming our ministry when we feel that it is unimportant or pointing us to the need for further teaching and healing.

Above all, this dialogue with Mark has pointed us to the need for mutual ministry. The story of Jesus and his followers cannot go on unless there are both those who proclaim and those who listen, those who heal and those who are being healed, those who teach and those who are open to teaching. What is most crucial about this kind of mutuality, however, is that official and unofficial ministry meet in the common need to receive as well as to give. When there is an openness to God's call, cultural patterns are subverted and real ministry happens in a variety of unexpected ways in the community. A dynamic interaction between official and unofficial ministry characterizes such an openness to the challenges that Jesus places before all of his followers.

Using the story of the followers of Jesus to describe several paradigms of ministry has not led us to an idealistic picture of official ministry. Instead, we have been invited to personal identification with the temptations, failures, and opportunities that came to two specific groups of disciples of Jesus. The narrative suggests that ministry is dynamic and changing as persons respond both by receiving the ministry of others and by willingly ministering to others in unexpected ways.

What this means for us as Mennonites in the midst of our particular social and political realities is not clearly outlined for us. However, as we struggle to name analogies to the Gospel story in the realities of our day, we too can be drawn into the writing of an official story that subverts cultural patterns. We too can discover a flexible and dynamic pattern of ministry. We too can overcome the fear that leads to rigid structures that paralyze our ministry. In this way the good news of Jesus will be proclaimed by both official and unofficial ministers working together in mutuality and trust.

Chapter Seven

Clarifying the Pastoral Role "On the Fly": The Praxis of Pastoral Ministry

Duane Beck

> Duane Beck served as a writer and steering committee member of the Pastorate Project, a churchwide program to clarify and support congregations and pastors in their mutual relationships. This essay grows out of his experience in ministry and his involvement in that project.

The pastor's role is finally clarified not in the classroom, nor by a book, but within the complexity and rigor of congregational life. A pastor can ricochet back and forth among the grief and funeral preparation of an unexpected death, the pain and denial of a sexual abuse case, a budget shortfall, a shortage of volunteer Sunday school teachers, and a conflict over music styles. All of this may be happening simultaneously with worship planning and sermon preparation!

In each situation the pastor picks up a different role, a different way of relating. Obviously, one role will not fit every situation. Neither will the culturally prominent roles of manager or therapist be appropriate in each case, nor will the more traditional role of preacher/teacher fit each situation. The pastor takes on a different *modus operandi* and a different way of relating in each circumstance. The effort of this chapter is not to promote an all-encompassing role definition but to help pastors simultaneously facing diverse situations think about how they might be present as persons and how they might best direct their energies and pastoral skills.

A fitting illustration of the process for choosing roles appropriate to the diverse pastoral tasks comes from my cousin who edited professional sports programs for national television in the Washington, D.C., area. During the Washington Redskins' football games, he and several editors and producers were squashed together in a semitrailer in front of many TV monitors. Each monitor represented one of the cameras on the field. My cousin had to make instant editing decisions about which TV angle to show the TV audience during the course of play. He called this "editing on the fly." That aptly describes what pastors need to do: clarify their pastoral role "on the fly," during the action, choosing which role to take up and which to lay down. Assuming and fulfilling these several pastoral roles has as its goal to communicate the presence and work of God through appropriate relationships and by careful directing of pastoral skills.

I. Accepting the Pastoral Role

A story: In my first ten years of pastoring, I greatly benefitted from regular consultation with a Clinical Pastoral Education supervisor. One day I came into his office frustrated with the church, saying, "They won't do this, they won't do that, they. . . they. . . ." His response probably is one of the reasons why I am still a pastor. He said, "You Mennonites believe in community, but I keep hearing the word 'they.' Duane, where are you in relation to the church? Aren't you part of the church too?" Bingo! His observations pointed out the dissonance between my belief about church and my pastoral actions and emotional response to congregational realities. That was the beginning of asking myself, "How do I lead this congregation as pastor while still remaining part of the community of believers?" It was an introductory lesson in clarifying my pastoral role "on the fly" within the living realities of church life. What are my responsibilities and how do I relate with these people as pastor?

What I did not realize then was that the consultant was guiding me through a dangerous intersection, the three-way intersection where the deeply spiritual vocational call meets congregational realities, which is then processed through the filter of the pastor's emotional system. A dark cloud had set in. On the surface I was struggling with the question, "How does the pastor who six months earlier took the vow 'to be a good minister of Jesus Christ by the grace of God' lead people who seemingly don't want to be led?" The consultant helped sharpen the question by asking me to think of leading this specific congregation with its own unique systemic qualities. And I needed to look at my internal emotional responses to gain a better understanding of my self.

When God calls a person to pastoral ministry, something deeply stirring, humbling, and terrifying takes place. As the church confirms God's call in ordination through the laying on of hands – loving, supporting, praying hands – something changes inside the pastor. But after the pivotal ordination moment has occurred, the "everydayness" of pastoring sets in. An internal dissonance develops. There is a clash between one's deeply spiritual vocational call and mundane pastoral tasks. The bulletin needs to be printed.

Pastoral visits seem not to develop a deeply spiritual dialogue but only seem to placate people's need for attention. Well-crafted sermons fall on deaf ears. Conflicts and sometimes petty differences need to be mediated. In some conflicted churches the pastor's own survival is a major task. I have wondered how pastors who take the ordination vow of "correctly handling the word of truth" spiritually guide people who read their bulletin during the holy worship moment of reading the Scripture?

This point where vocational call meets congregational realities is a dangerous intersection. This is where the pastoral role must be clarified. There are no detours around this intersection. It must be navigated.

Some pastors wreck. They become disillusioned with the church, or they are plagued with self-doubt about their gifts and call. The spiritual infilling and congregational support so evident at ordination seemingly evaporates. The pastor's vision dims.

Other pastors find navigating this dangerous intersection an opportunity for pastoral and personal growth. It is a challenge to integrate their faith, vocational call, and emotional patterns with congregational realities. They learn to clarify their pastoral role "on the fly," both in the midst of their own internal emotional response and within the context of external congregational forces. And ultimately they trust that the weaving together of God, the church, and the person is how the tapestry of the pastoral role is made.

I have attempted to show reasons why it is helpful for pastors to clearly choose the roles they assume in diverse situations. Below I will look more carefully at the ingredients that go into the mix of clarifying these diverse pastoral roles.

II. Clarifying the Pastoral Role

The pastoral role is best described, I believe, as the "internal regulating principle inside oneself that enables one, as a person, to manage what one does in relation to [the congregational setting]."[1] The "internal regulating principle" is like a gyroscope (before the age of computers) that served to keep an airplane on an even keel and going in the right direction in turbulent weather. In pastoral turbulence such as that caused by an infant's

---

[1] *Professional Management*; Notes Prepared by Grubb Institute on Concepts and Relationships for Professional Management, 1988.

sudden death, a budget shortfall, or conflicts over music styles, what enables pastors to keep equilibrium and to direct their energies and skills so as not to lose sight of the larger purpose and vision of the church? This requires an ability to "clarify on the fly" by finding those helpful ways to relate and by directing one's energies appropriately.

To "clarify on the fly," pastors must do two things: (1) consider their person or self as a pastor, and (2) understand the mission of the congregation. Job descriptions, while helpful in mapping out general pastoral expectations, are inadequate in helping a pastor relate and choose responsible action in the demands of the moment. The job description defines what one does, but not how one does it. There is a difference.

The expectations people have of a pastor do not define the pastoral role, but they are quite powerful, nevertheless. I have been seduced at times into internalizing other people's expectations, particularly critical people. At those times my inner need to be accepted by everyone was the internal principle that regulated my energies and actions. Since we live and act out of our internal regulating principles all the time, a key to making good pastoral choices is a growing self-awareness. For instance, in becoming self-aware, I need to ask myself: "Is my specific response to critical comments based on the internal emotional gyroscopes of self-doubt, or anger, or fear of conflict? Or is it motivated by furthering the purpose of the church?"

III. The "Geography" of Pastoral Role

Speaking metaphorically, the pastoral role has a lot to do with geography, the pastor's own inner landscape as well as the geography of the congregation and their place together within the Kingdom of God. The pastor's inner landscape that affects how we relate and take up pastoral responsibilities is made up of several parts; particularly key are the pastor's emotional and spiritual beings. Edwin Friedman writes that . . .

> all clergymen and clergywomen . . . are simultaneously
> involved in three distinct families whose emotional forces
> interlock: the families within the congregation, our
> congregations (as a corporate family) and our own (family).
> Because the emotional process in all these systems is
> identical, unresolved issues in any one of them can produce

symptoms in the others, and increased understanding of any one creates more effective functioning in all three.[2]

How the pastor's family system dealt with stress, co-dependency, conflict, failure, success, authority, and how the family expressed its sexuality, anger, and grace will greatly influence the pastor's emotional responses within the system of the congregational family. Consequently, as pastors become more aware of their family system, they will more clearly be able to choose their pastoral responses to a given situation rather than reacting out of past emotionality.

The pastor's spiritual self is foundational to pastoral relationships and pastoral leadership. To be in touch with our unique spiritual journey helps us know the roots, the strength, and the movement of God's Spirit out of which we incarnate and mediate God to others. Learning the map of one's spiritual geography might consider the following:

A. Taking time to examine one's past experiences of God's grace – noting the experiences of forgiveness, healing, and the process of renewal in one's life.

B. Noting our encounter with God's salvation – the uniquely personal kinds of slavery out of which God has called one, and of the power of Jesus Christ that continually gives spiritual protection and enables one to withstand temptation.

C. Remembering the formative effects of people and the church on our life – these experiences with God's people shape our present vision of church life and leadership responses.

D. Being aware of the incarnational nature of our ministry as we explore the nature of our current relationship with Jesus Christ; our awareness of the movements of grace and healing in our lives; our experience of temptation, sin, forgiveness, and spiritual protection; the unique gifting and empowering by the Holy Spirit; and our practice of prayer and other spiritual disciplines.

Of course, the pastoral role is not defined by the pastor's inner self alone. Congregational geography shapes the pastoral role much as the predominate southerly Kansas winds shape trees to lean northward. The congregation where pastors "live, move, and have their being" has a place

---

[2]Edwin Friedman, *Generation to Generation* (New York: The Guilford Press, 1985), p. 1.

and time, a history and tradition, a theology and practice. The pastoral role is finally shaped among people with whom one pastors. This, of course, is as it should be.

To map congregational geography, the pastor needs to pay particular attention to two things, both of which are significant in defining the pastoral role: the "containing system" and the "purposive system" of the congregation. The "containing system" is a way of viewing the dynamics of relationships contained within the congregation, and it is most often referred to as "Family Systems."[3] The containing system, with its emphasis on relationships, helps the pastor to pay attention to relationships within the congregation.

The purposive system focuses on congregational mission and thus deals with the interaction of congregational geography and kingdom geography. The location of the kingdom is where God is working to unite all things together in Christ as head of the kingdom of God. The purpose or mission of the congregation is to understand and carry out its slice of kingdom work in its specific location. What is going on in the environment in which the congregation lives? What are the resources of the congregation that enable it to do what God calls it to do within that environment?

In reality, there is often a difference between the intended purpose and what actually happens in a congregation. Taking up pastoral roles to further the purpose of the church is crucial; discerning mission, keeping the mission vision alive, and helping the church to do its intended mission is part of leadership work. Therefore, it is most necessary for pastors to direct their energies and skills to further the purpose of the congregation. The pastor's priorities should reflect the congregational purpose. It boils down to the mundane tasks of scheduling the daily and weekly "to do lists," meetings, and attending to the relationships that further the congregation's purpose.

According to systems' theory, as pastors become clear about what they do to further the church's mission, then other leaders will become more clear about what they are to do as well. Clarifying pastoral roles creates a snowball effect that enables clarity of life and mission within the congregation.

---

[3]Family Systems theory has been championed by such people as therapist Murray Bowen. Edwin Friedman in *Generation to Generation* helps pastors apply the theory to the congregation.

IV. Summary

Clarifying the pastoral role is similar to the art of juggling. The many dynamics that enter into taking up the pastoral role are constantly moving. Many camera angles show the entire field of congregational life, and one angle presents the best picture of pastoral relationships and work at a moment in time. This is not to complicate role clarity. Rather, it is to say that the roles pastors choose express profoundly the interaction of God, pastor, and congregation. As pastors we need to pay particular attention to that interaction. Through it we discover the grace of our Lord Jesus Christ at work.

Chapter Eight

Re-institutionalizing the Pastorate:
A Proposal for Attracting More Able Candidates to Pastoral Ministry in Two Mennonite Denominations

Ardean L. Goertzen

The following essay was originally a part of a position paper written by Ardean Goertzen for the Pastorate Project, a churchwide program to clarify and support congregations and pastors in their mutual relationships.

I. Fundamental Dimension: Pastoral Roles and the Pastoral Role

This is a tough area to address, because in seeking to clarify and focus what pastors are to be and do with down-to-earth and practical suggestions, there are larger systemic dimensions that need to be kept in view. These systemic dimensions are enormously complex. What I believe we can offer at this stage is a framework for how to think about pastoral tasks or functions and the pastoral role in a congregational context. The choice of the word "roles" (plural) and "role" (singular) in the heading is deliberate. I am not assuming that what needs to be clarified is limited only to roles or tasks. That would be taking an overly functionalist view of the pastorate and, by that, play into the very nature of the problem that is systemic in our midst. What also needs to be clarified is who pastors are to be and also what they are to do. Both need to be spelled out in terms of the framework offered here.

In terms of the Christian movement and faith, we are dealing with a unique God (Yahweh who reveals Himself most fully in Jesus Christ) who calls into being a unique people (Israel and the new Israel) and calls into being a unique role to lead His people in mission and ministry. These three uniquenesses need to be held together in a holistic way. Such a holistic view has implications in several areas, such as our understanding of: (A) The call of the pastor, (B) The identity of the pastor, (C) A sense of the uniqueness of the pastoral role, (D) The indicators of depth understanding and practice that embodies this uniqueness. A brief outline of these four dimensions is offered here.

A. The Call of the Pastor

A sense of being chosen by God to be a pastoral leader is fundamental. Whether it's Moses, Isaiah, or Jesus, each accepts the role of servant, the chief characteristic, since each is willing to accept delegation from God to be what God wishes him/her to be on God's behalf. Their vocation initially depends not upon worthiness, spirituality, or acceptability, but solely upon their being chosen by God as his representative. Our day has seen a marked erosion in this kind of sense of call from God. Robert Bellah has noted that part of what is endemic in American life is the substitution of a sense of lively vocation by a more determined career, which is planned by a calculus of success and individual fulfillment. This is true even of the pastoral vocation.

The pastoral vocation is more than a job or list of routine duties to be carried out. The pastor is a symbol and representative of God and the things pertaining to God, and is not just a practitioner. Briefly put, the call to pastor comes from "above" as a gift from God and from "below" as it is tested and verified through practice in the congregation. The call from "above" and from "below" create a tension that can increase creativity if handled right. If not, it can also mean big trouble. There needs to be both a clear Christian identity and a clear pastoral identity.

B. The Identity of the Pastor

Identity is intimately related to call. Serious faith formation must articulate a uniqueness or there is no identity, for identity is being able to distinguish who is "me" and who is "not me." What this implies is that there is an important boundary that pastors must be keenly aware of and that needs to be managed. The data from my research would support the conclusion that the better the pastor manages the boundary of his/her distinctiveness or uniqueness, the more it helps members to sharpen their distinctiveness or uniqueness.

Being able to manage such a boundary with competence requires a great deal of differentiation from family of origin. Edwin Friedman, in his book *Generation to Generation*, expounds on this at great length. His point is that a systems view and differentiation from family of origin help pastors not to get hooked into emotional triangles and the like. Rather, it helps them to understand their position in the congregation by understanding better their position in their family of origin. The basic concept of leadership when viewed from the perspective of self-differentiation is this: "If a leader will take primary responsibility for his or her own position as "head" and work to define his or her own goals and self, while staying in touch with the rest of the organism, there is a more than reasonable chance that the body will follow."[1]

In a summary way, we can suggest the following principles that a Christian (and I believe we can say professional) pastor needs to exhibit:

–A clear Christian identity.

–An extensive and reflective understanding of what constitutes that identity.

–A self-consciousness how that Christian identity shapes perception of the present congregational and concrete world-historical situation.

–A wise discernment of the implications of this Christian perception for action.

–A clear pastoral identity.

–A person's sense of call to pastor must be clear and affirmed; the pastor must be able to say with heart, mind and soul, "I want to be a pastor," and mean it to the marrow of their bones. (This does not mean that there is no room for doubt or arguing with God about one's call such as is witnessed in the life and ministry of the prophet Jeremiah.)

–A genuine sense of the uniqueness of the pastoral role as outlined below.

C. A Sense of the Uniqueness of the Pastoral Role

A deep sense of vocation as noted above is fundamental. In my project report, *Congregational Systemic Stress and Pastoral Burnout*, I proposed that ". . . the clearer pastors become about their role as it relates to a specific congregation, the clearer members will be about their roles, both in the congregation and in the world of work. This would be the case not because of good modeling by pastors, but when pastors are free to carry out

---

[1]Edwin Friedman, *Generation to Generation* (New York: The Guilford Press, 1985), p. 229.

their role with clarity and conviction, members will be free to be different and take up their role as they choose."[2]

The uniqueness of the pastoral role is related to a call from God that implies at least the following: It is very much a public role with tradition-specific expectations bound up with a role that has to be taken seriously and worked with creatively. The pastor is, in a sense, an eschatological figure, which means that he/she is someone who embodies ends and is not caught up simply in means or technique. It is one thing to be a member and yet quite another thing to carry the weight of the congregation's symbolic meaning in an institutionalized role as pastor. Because of the public and eschatological nature of the role, the pastor is and can be a very powerful symbolic presence. Following from the above, pastors are representatives of the Holy and divine in life. They embody what Christian churches choose to affirm by way of values and mode of being in the world.

D. The Indicators of Depth Understanding and Practice

There are several areas in which we need to begin to look for indicators that a depth sense of the uniqueness of the being and role of the pastor is understood and being embodied in practice.

First, there would be the area of the person or sense of self. To know one's "self" is vital and essential. Being in touch with one's body and feelings is important for the ability to reflect carefully on all areas of one's involvement in life and ministry. A good hermeneutic of personality is also helpful. But more than this, a key indicator would be the competency (which implies skills) to stay deeply immersed in life and ministry while at the same time oscillating between objective and subjective perspectives.

Pastors need to stay as deeply immersed in life/ministry situations as possible and not to withdraw or become detached. That is the goal. This is what Friedman means by staying in touch with the congregational body. The real trick, and it is unbelievably difficult, is to move back and forth between subjective perspectives (being in touch or aware of feelings, images, thoughts, and intimations/intuitions), and then moving with all of that to the objective pole. At the objective pole the pastor processes these feelings, images, and intuitions by putting them through a cognitive grid that includes theological categories as well as systemic ones. This is what is meant by oscillating

---

[2]Ardean Goertzen, *Congregational Systemic Stress and Pastoral Burnout* (published by the author, 1987) p. 51.

between subjective and objective perspectives. Such oscillation becomes impossible if the pastor withdraws or becomes detached.

This means a willingness on the part of pastors to subject themselves to stress. But to allow ourselves to be subjected to stress in relation to our environment can therefore be a positive condition for the transformation of that environment. Oscillation as described above, then, becomes a way to manage stress – not manage stress out of existence, but to anticipate it. It is also to use one's experience of it to develop greater insight into the way systems function, and to possess a better understanding of relations between people and between people and God. Secondly, the pastor would be able to demonstrate the ability to think theologically about personal, congregational, community, and historical events. This would mean using both perceptual and interpretive skills. Biblical and historical perspectives would also be included in this.

Thirdly, the pastor would be able to demonstrate the ability to listen and think systemically. This would include global and community thinking. What all would be involved in a good hermeneutic of systems and culture is something that needs further thought.

II. Introduction on the Pastoral Role

The concepts of person-role-system form the basis for my thinking about tasks. The model we are proposing here must not be only of a conceptual kind but point to what we want to promote as a heuristic (learning) mode. Systems thinking is one such heuristic tool and it is much needed. My assumption is that congregations are unique organisms and organizations, and that no model can anticipate all the kinds of functions that might be called for. On-the-job learning or contextual learning is of the essence.

What we are aiming for is to assist pastors to take authority in role as it relates to the congregation as system, through the process of framing or reframing their experience of the context in which they live and work systemically.

Pastors will make or re-fashion their role as they learn to "read" the congregation as system. This means that the notion of role is a tremendously dynamic one and that the tasks will vary from one time and place to another. This is another way of saying that discerning what God's will and calling are in relation to a given congregation is something that involves constant attention and struggle. This also means that pastors: (A) be open to receiving the projections of members in the congregation and work with that as prime material, (B) be results oriented rather than program oriented, and (C) be confident in what they represent as pastors.

Governing Principle Number One: The priority of the pastor's time and energy must be determined by careful discernment about what is congruent with and affirms the pastor's own sense of divine call and authentic conception of the work role.

This principle is another way of saying that pastors need to be true to their calling first of all. If there is neither freedom nor the courage available to say a definite "No" to some things, it will ultimately mean the curtailment of the freedom of members as well. The seductive power of the routine is as dangerous in pastoral ministry as any other organization, perhaps more so. Freedom from the routine is critical if there is to be freedom for such things as taking authority to manage, modify, or transform the pastor's own relatedness to the system or systems in which pastors live and work. The receiving mode of existence on the part of pastors needs to be guarded at all costs. Prayer, contemplation, and meditation need to have a central place in the pastor's life. Meditative thinking is a style of thinking which is synthetic, imaginative, holistic, and metaphorical; it seeks by imagination and intuition to grasp the webs of significance that hold the meaning of the people in the congregation and beyond.

Governing Principle Number Two: The priority of the pastor's time and energy should focus primarily on working with the congregation as a whole and key subgroups within it rather than one-on-one work with individuals.

This principle is another way of saying that systemic ways of working are primary. This is not to say that working with individuals is totally cut out or out of place. It's more a matter of keeping the whole in view when working with individuals. For example, are offerings clues about what is going on in the congregation at a systemic level, i.e., are they a mouthpiece for a large segment or group within the congregation as a whole?

Governing Principle Number Three: The priority of the pastor's time and energy will be given to leadership rather than to management.

Here again, we are not saying that pastors do not need to do any managing. But there is an important distinction here that needs to be kept clear. As Warren Bennis has clearly stated: "...leading does not mean management; the difference between the two is crucial. There are many institutions I know that are very well managed and very poorly led. They may excel in the ability to handle all the routine inputs each day, yet they may never ask whether the routine should be preserved at all."[3] Leading is more a matter of the ability to attract followers in task performance. Attracting them lies in the further ability to look ahead and offer vision, maintaining a keen spiritual perspective on life and ministry, asking the right questions about mission and ministry, and being able to conceptualize the overarching goals and tasks.

The point is to keep clearly in mind that the church is both a divine organism and a human institution. There is a real tension between the unique, transcendent nature of the church as an organization established by Christ, "managed" by God, and empowered by the continuing presence of the Holy Spirit, and the equally real nature of the church as a human organization, made up of fallible and sinful people, subject to the same human dynamics, problems, and needs as all other organizations.

Consider some further important points on leadership. Leaders have a significant role in creating a state of mind or climate of opinion in the congregation that is conducive to growth and development. Leaders have a significant role in creating an environment or the conditions most conducive to positive change, growth and development. Leaders embody and express the values that the church chooses to affirm, and that reality helps to hold the congregation together. Leaders conceive and articulate goals and ideals that lift people out of petty preoccupations and carry them above the conflicts that might, at least potentially, tear the congregation apart. Leaders articulate an urgent mission vision that unites people in the pursuit of objectives worthy of their best efforts and their human/Godly potential. Leaders work as a catalyst to energize, activate, organize, delegate, and train members to help bring congregational goals to reality. Leaders generally live with the whole "catholic" church in mind.

III. General Guidelines on Pastoral Functioning

From the more general principles outlined above we move now to more specific guidelines of pastoral functioning. What is outlined here may not seem reasonable to expect of pastors. However, as Christians and pastors we are asked to take our share of suffering, laying down our lives for each other. And for pastors this means a willingness to bear the weight of being in

---

[3]Warren Bennis, *The Unconscious Conspiracy*, "Why Leaders Can't Lead" (Redding, Massachusetts, Addison-Wesley, 1969) p. 154 and passim.

a public and institutionalized role with many and varied expectations attached to that role. Whether such things are reasonable depends on our attitude and perspective. From the standpoint of the "secular mind," such things might very well be unreasonable. We need to keep our expectations high regarding ministry and leadership on the one hand, and clear and focused on the other. Since each congregation is unique, the areas of functioning explained below cannot hope to cover every situation. So what is laid out here is a way of pointing to the ideal. We must realize that many adaptations will need to be made in concrete situations.

What I believe we want to affirm here is that pastors give their time to those areas that affirm what is central to the Christian faith tradition and that which is central in their education at seminary. Theological leadership would affirm the uniqueness of God, the church, the tradition, the Bible as divinely inspired and the leader as called by God. This section will explain what is meant by theological leadership (keeping in mind the distinction between leadership and management) in three areas: (A) Leading in the ministry of the liturgy, (B) Leading in the ministry of the Word, (C) Leading in the ministry of the rites/ordinances.

A. Leading the Ministry of the Liturgy. The grounding for this I have come to see as related very much to the priestly task of the pastor. I am very much in agreement with Larsen and Shopshire and their conclusion about worship and liturgy: "More and more we are realizing that worship, both corporate and private, is the sustaining energy for mission." For one, the liturgical movement with all of its riches, is effectively reminding us of the various dimensions of pastoral ministry, and that pastor/priest and people are brought by one Spirit into one Body. What is envisioned here is an understanding of the pastor as one who leads in setting forth the symbols, myths, stories, and language-lines of that eschatological treasure chest entrusted to the church.

This means that in terms of worship, the pastoral role is that of prompter. The pastor-as-prompter has the lines: i.e., s/he is a steward of the language of the Gospel. This view sees the church as a parent who gives the people a sacred language. This language is critical in helping members to look at the world Christ-like, to begin to adopt the "mind of Christ." In addition to creating a climate for people to enter into a worshipful mood or attitude (symbolic-activity), the proper conducting of the lines (gospel language) helps to create an environment in which positive change, growth and faith development can occur.[4]

The role of the pastor-as-prompter is accomplished through the following three sub-tasks: (1) to assist worshipers and prospective worshipers to manage their transition from work-activity to symbolic-activity in worship, (2) to provide opportunities for them to worship God, (3) to provide opportunities for them to make the transition back from symbolic-activity to work-activity.[5]

As Reed goes on to suggest, the paramount skill of the pastor/priest is to be aware of and sensitive to the process, whether consciously or unconsciously. S/he can then sympathize with the weak and rejoice in the strength of the free.

> "He will know the power of ritual to evoke symbols and discharge feelings, and be able to lead it so that worshipers can be without distractions in worshipping God. Above all else he needs to appreciate the place of dependence in life and be able to work with people in a dependent condition. Without these basic skills and insights he will only misuse the treasures of the Christian movement. With them, he can appreciate and set forth the symbolic language and actions of the apostolic faith for the support, guidance and enrichment of the worshipers."[6]

In a summary way, we can say that the view of corporate worship presented here views

> "God as the giver of inscrutable grace and is the audience to whom we offer our praise and prayer. The pastor, as representing the living tradition of the church, gives us the language - the lines - which enable us to participate in God's ongoing activity in the world. As the actors we are called to

---

[4]C. John Weborg and Inagrace T. Dietterich, *Corporate Worship (Chicago: Center for Parish Development, 1988)*, pp. 19-26.

[5]Bruce Reed, *The Dynamics of Religion: Process and Movement in Christian Churches (London: Darton, Longman and Todd Ltd.*, 1978), p. 169.

[6]Ibid., pp. 170f.

see the whole of our lives as "liturgy" – as service to God in fulfillment of divine purposes."[7]

B. Leading the Ministry of the Word. This area of functioning is closely related to liturgy discussed above. As envisioned here, it means the pastor-as-preacher and the pastor-as-teacher. The role of the pastor-as-preacher is to stand on the boundary between the worship service and the environment from which the worshippers come and to which they will go, and from that vantage point to provide an interpretive word that is "a word in season" that helps transform and give authority to the symbols and stories of the Christian tradition. The preacher gives the symbols, myths, and stories of the Christian movement authority by showing how they comprehend the depths of the human predicament. When this is accomplished, it can affect the hearer's perceptions and judgments, hopefully in a direction that is more congruent with the values of the gospel.

The task of education, which has often been missing almost entirely as a continuing thread in the fabric of the ministry of the ordained, may offer critical guidance and information that facilitates community or unity in the body of Christ. There are several ways that sound theological education could provide for this. Some of these ways would be to provide for a common sense of identity, for a common authority, for a common memory, for a common vision, for a common shared life together in community, for a common shared life together in service to the world.

Now the tough question: Can a pastor do all that is required in the area of theological leadership with dynamic competence, vigor, and skill? A pastor needs to have a profound sense of the overall role and tasks involved in preaching, teaching, and leading worship. This would include a sense of the symbolic and the sacramental in all of worship and life.

C. Leading in the Ministry of the Rites/Sacraments/Ordinances. In this case, we are dealing not only with rites of intensification as represented by celebration of the Lord's Supper or the Eucharist but also with rites of initiation and assimilation that properly belong to the people. These rites of initiation have to do with transition points in the life cycle events of people.

The role of the pastor as ritual elder or leader of the ministry of the ordinances is to offer a framework for meaning in life at the transition points by assisting, guiding, enabling, and interpreting at the boundary between the church and its local human environment. When people come for baptisms,

---

[7]C. John Weborg and Inagrace Dietterich, *op cit,* p. 36.

weddings, or funerals, they come to the church not for management but for opportunity. What needs regulation is the interchange between the people concerned and the social, psychological, and familial environments in which they are set. The church and its pastors serve that process.

Carr suggests that pastors revolt against a role assigned to them because they confuse in their thinking two separable systems in church life. There is, on the one hand, its public ministry (the access system) of which they are part, which provides these access points for people with their dependencies. On the other hand, there is the support system, by which all who witness to the Christian faith, wherever they may be, are encouraged and enabled to be the church.

As a Christian, the minister is also part of this system. If, however, pastors attempt to make the support system into the access system by trying to delegate the rites or occasional offices to the laity, they are usually disappointed. The very stress they are seeking to reduce by such delegation is increased instead. This is because they have overlooked the nature of human expectations, and in so doing, will be closing down access points for the parishioners and confusing the church members. Everyone then begins to feel incompetent. I'm sure there may be room for debate on this.

Chapter Nine

An Emerging Theology of Ministry: Incarnational Presence

Marcus Smucker

Marcus Smucker wrote this essay during a sabbatical leave from Associated Mennonite Biblical Seminary of Elkhart, Indiana. It reflects his unique perspective as one who forged his understanding of ministry from within the pastorate and now teaches pastoral theology within the seminary, thus combining both praxis and theological reflection within an academic context.

I. Introduction

This is a theology of ministry as it emerged in my own experience as a pastor and pastoral counselor. I begin with autobiographical reflections on experiences that helped shape my practice of ministry followed by reflections on some of the implicit theology underlying my work as a pastoral person.

In writing this, I am conscious of the dialogue in the Mennonite church since the sixties concerning the nature of pastoral ministry in relationship to the ministry of all in the church. Since my understanding of ministry was forged on the anvil of pastoral experience, the focus of this statement is primarily on pastoral ministry. Toward the end, I comment briefly upon the relationship between the ministry of all who are baptized and the office of pastoral ministry.

In the history of the Mennonite church there has been a plurality of ministers with various patterns of congregational leadership, e.g., bishops, elders, deacons, pastors, etc. Today much of this is encompassed under the rubric of pastoral ministry which includes various aspects of leadership and ministry in the congregation. In the Mennonite context, ministry may engage the gifts and time of several persons commissioned to leadership as well as those who are more formally called to the pastoral "office." Even though the ministry patterns may vary in different settings, the inherent nature of pastoral ministry remains the same.

Therefore, when I allude to "the pastor" in this writing, I am referring to the role of pastoral ministry in the congregation. It must be understood that the characteristics of ministry described in this statement normally require the time and attention of a plurality of leaders; ministry in the congregation is greater than the gifts and energy of any one person.

This statement on ministry is limited, from the perspective of a more comprehensive theology, because it is essentially Christological in focus. However, since discipleship (following Jesus) is crucial to Mennonite theology, Christology seems to be an appropriate point of beginning for a Mennonite theology of ministry. Certainly this perspective has been a vital foundation for my own practice of ministry over the years.

II. Autobiographical Reflections: Emerging Understandings of Ministry

As a young pastor, I struggled for several years to find my identity and purpose in ministry. I pondered about the role of pastor in the congregation. Who am I when preaching in the pulpit? Who am I when making pastoral visits and what are these visits to accomplish? What shall my voice and influence be in decision making in the congregation? Do I as pastor have a greater responsibility than others for the life and well-being of the congregation? What is to guide me in my understanding of pastoral ministry?

I soon became aware that even though I had no prior experience, the congregation could not help me articulate my purpose and identity as a pastor. They knew there were tasks for me to do, but they had no clear sense of mission, let alone an understanding of my role in it. My seminary studies provided training in certain pastoral functions but did not provide me with a coherent theology of ministry to help me understand who I was to be and why.

This crisis of identity was heightened by the inner-city context of my ministry. It seemed clear to me that our congregation was to minister to the city. The needs of our neighborhood were great, and there was no end of possibilities and requests for service and care. But as I began to lead the congregation in urban ministries, I soon encountered sharp criticism from within our conference district for not focusing more exclusively on evangelism. Some said I was engaging in a social gospel.

This nudged me to more fully examine my reasons for leading our congregation in service ministries in our neighborhood of poverty. Why should we help sponsor a halfway house for released prisoners or develop programs for delinquent teenagers and isolated elderly along with organizing neighborhood Bible studies and inviting people to worship with us? Was this being done in faithfulness to Jesus Christ, or was I simply acting as a liberal "do-gooder"?

As I sought anew to comprehend the implications of the gospel for our congregational life, the core of my understanding of ministry began to emerge. I began to develop a theology of ministry through my understanding of Christology. I observed that Jesus ministered to people in their immediate need, and as they were ready to hear, he also taught them about God. It seemed reasonable to believe the risen Christ still comes to people as they are, and the ministry of Christ begins with the need at hand. Indeed, Jesus declared himself to be present with the destitute and needy (Matthew 25). I concluded that although the ultimate mission of Jesus is to lead people to communion with God (Revelation 3:20), he also ministered to people in need, regardless of the outcome.

Since Christ was God's incarnate presence to all, I, as a minister of the gospel, am also to be a presence (John 17:18) in the name of Christ to any person, group, or situation to which I am called. The presence of the living Christ is to become incarnate through me and through the community of Christians everywhere. This understanding of incarnational presence became the heart of my own theology of ministry.

The concept of presence has been further illuminated by my reflections on the priestly work of Christ. In his priestly role, Jesus sought to foster reconciliation and communion in the divine-human encounter. Even as Jesus addressed humans in behalf of God and prayed to God in behalf of humans, so I am called to be an agent of God. As a Christian and a minister of the gospel, I am to "incarnate" the presence of God to those with whom I sojourn, and to speak to God in behalf of others.

This informs the core of my work as a pastor, pastoral counselor, professor, and spiritual director. To remind me of this, I have a picture of the praying hands above the chair where people sit when they come to my office at Associated Mennonite Biblical Seminary. When I am most in tune with my calling, I am aware of the presence of God as I meet with people; not only am I to help incarnate God's presence with others but also to receive that presence through those who come. God wants to become known through each of us as we meet and relate. To minister to one another is to help incarnate the presence of God to one another.

The nature and content of this incarnational presence has been informed and developed in my thought and experience by several key metaphors from Scripture and human experience. These metaphors, which also help provide an understanding of pastoral ministry, include the priest, the shepherd, the helper[1], the midwife[2], and "the body of Christ."

"Priest" informs my core sense of whom I am to be in ministry. "Shepherd" provides a basis for understanding the relationship between responsibility and authority for pastoral care. The "Helper" or advocate helps define the nature of ministry. "Midwife" informs me that God is the originator and sustainer of life, so as a minister I am not the creator or bearer of life, but am called to attend to the spiritual birthing and growth process in others. The "body of Christ" metaphor helps establish the context for ministry, the communal nature of the role of the pastor. The ecclesial context of ministry helps shape the meaning, purpose, and means for how ministry is to occur in the church.

These metaphors of presence help provide character and content to the concept of incarnational presence. They have helped to shape my own thought and practice and are important to the development of a theological rationale for ministry.

III. Biblical/Theological Reflections: An Emerging Theology of Ministry

A. The Minister as Presence

Jesus was called Emmanuel, "God with us" (Matthew 1:23). This is the heart of the incarnation. As God's presence was made known to Israel, in a cloud by day and a pillar of fire by night, so God's presence was made known to us through the incarnate Jesus. Through the incarnation God has come to "tabernacle" with us until the end of time. God has come for self-disclosure, to identify with us, to be reconciled with us, and to transform our lives.

---

[1]This comes from the Greek term *paraklatos*, which is used of the Holy Spirit in John 13-17 and also in 1 John 2:1.

[2]Over a period of several years, female students in the pastoral leadership classes at Associated Mennonite Biblical Seminary helped me understand the meaning and significance of midwife as a vital metaphor for ministry. Later this was reinforced by some of my readings in spiritual direction. One particularly important book describing this is by Margaret Guenther, *Holy Listening: The Art of Spiritual Direction* (Boston: Covley Publications, 1992).

God seeks self-disclosure. Paul declared that in Jesus "the whole fullness of deity dwells bodily" (Colossians 2:9, NRSV). Jesus revealed the true nature of God – immanent and transcendent, mysterious and holy, correcting and compassionate, one who loves us and seeks covenant relationship. God desires to become known to us through the incarnation.

God identifies with us. Jesus became like us "in every respect" to identify with the experience of being human. Clothed in flesh and blood, Jesus encountered temptation, finitude, death, and resurrection so that he can lead us through our encounters with life and death and new life. In Jesus, God identifies with a broken world.

God longs for reconciliation with us. "In Christ, God was reconciling the world to himself, not counting their trespasses against them" (2 Corinthians 5:19). Jesus came to set us free from bondage and to help us to live in peace. The ministry of Jesus through his life, death, and resurrection is God's appeal to us to be reconciled and to receive forgiveness and salvation.

God intends to transform our lives. If we receive God's offer of forgiveness and salvation, our lives will be changed. Anyone who is in Christ is a new creation, the old has passed away, everything becomes new (2 Corinthians 5:17). The shape of this transformation is apparent in the life and teachings of Jesus. The power for transformation comes from the risen Christ in our midst.

This then is the nature of God's incarnate presence: self-disclosure, identification, reconciliation, and transformation. This presence continues to be expressed through the body of Christ (John 17:18). As God was incarnate in Jesus, so God is now incarnate in the body of Christ, the people of God. We who have been reconciled and transformed become part of the means and message of reconciliation and transformation for others in the world. To witness to God's presence among us is the foundation for ministry. All Christian ministry is rooted in this incarnational presence which seeks to foster encounter with the divine.

God's presence may be experienced through human encounter. Indeed, humans are able to be present with one another through empathy, mutuality, identification, and caring for one another. While such experiences may be instrumental, they are not adequate in themselves to express the presence of the divine in human experience. This presence is a unique work of the Spirit. Humans participate in God's presence through spiritual discernment that acknowledges when and how God is present, faith that sees what is not yet evident, and solidarity with God's self-disclosing, reconciling, and transforming intent.

Such participation with God is foundational to all Christian ministry and to the "office" of the pastor. The pastor is called to nurture awareness and receptivity to this presence among the people of God. Therefore, a sense of participation in the incarnational presence is fundamental to an understanding of pastoral ministry. The theology implicit in these metaphors of presence – priest, shepherd, helper, midwife, and body of Christ – can enhance the self-understanding and function of pastoral ministry.

B. The Minister as Priest

The ministry of Jesus was priestly at its core. Jesus became like us in every respect "so that he might be a merciful and faithful high priest in the service of God" (Hebrews 2:17-18). As priest, Jesus speaks to humanity on behalf of God and to God on behalf of humans. Jesus reveals God's true nature of love, compassion, grace, redemptive desire, and judgment. He represents our needs and concerns to God, interceding in our behalf so that we might be reconciled to God and be delivered from evil (Hebrews 7:24).

The priestly role is at the core of the incarnation event. There is no greater or more tender concern than this: to be instrumental in the fruitful encounter between God and humans. Therefore, it is also at the core of all Christian ministry.[3] The body of Christ is called to participate in this priestly function as it seeks to represent God's interests and joins in God's mission in the world.

The pastor has a particular call to facilitate the encounter between God and the people. As an agent of God, the pastor nurtures and facilitates the expression of the priestly function within the body of Christ. As an agent of God, the pastor calls all to be reconciled to God.

The priestly metaphor is fundamental to the understanding and practice of pastoral care, including pastoral counseling and spiritual direction. These crucial roles of healing, correcting, guiding, and spiritual discovery must always be done with a clear vision for the priestly nature of this work. Pastors who participate in this expression of incarnational presence must remain aware of the instrumental nature of their calling and not assume

---

[3]Obviously there was historic significance to the ministry of Jesus who made atonement for our sins. This is not to suggest that we are just as Jesus was, but it is to suggest that we participate in the salvific work Jesus came to do on earth.

inappropriate authority nor fail to adequately communicate the word God has for those whom they serve.

C. The Minister as Shepherd

Since the term pastor is derived from the word shepherd, this metaphor is important in understanding the nature of pastoral ministry. Indeed, shepherd is a key metaphor for ministry in the Old Testament (Psalm 23, Jeremiah 23, Ezekiel 34), in the teachings of Jesus (John 10), in the church (1 Peter 5:1-4) and in early Anabaptist thought (Schleitheim Confession). The image of God as shepherd in Psalm 23 is a reflection of the character of God and the certainty of God with us.[4]

As is true with many metaphors, the image of pastor as shepherd has particular characteristics that are relevant for a theology of ministry. John M. Fowler very aptly says,

> "The metaphor of a shepherd and a sheep is not intended to convey the image of wisdom over stupidity, power over weakness, order over chaos, certainty over helplessness; for in the arena of the flock of God, both shepherd and sheep are made of the same substance, and therefore it behooves the shepherd to watch out against the perils of abusive power. The metaphor is meant to urge a relationship of love and care that the shepherd is to have toward"[5] those being served.

There are various roles that readily emerge from the shepherding metaphor that are relevant for pastoral ministry today. Some of these will be pursued here under the rubric of: the pastor as watchperson, the pastor as one who exercises authority, the pastor as minister of the Word, the pastor as caregiver, and the pastor as one who is trustworthy.

1. The Pastor as Watchperson

Shepherds are called to assume responsibility for the welfare of God's people (Jeremiah 23, Ezekiel 34, John 10). They are to feed the sheep,

---

[4]Shepherd is a role that encompasses other roles such as prophet, priest, and king; such leaders were to shepherd the people. This is a journey and survival metaphor with the image of the shepherd leading out in the morning to find food and water, gathering, protecting, correcting, healing, restoring so the sheep can make the journey and experience well-being.

[5] *Ministry: International Journal for Pastors*, November 1994, p. 5.

strengthen the weak, heal the sick, bind up the injured, and bring back those who have gone astray (Ezekiel 34). They must lead according to God's Word, seek God's counsel, seek the lost, speak the truth, gather, protect, deal wisely, and execute justice (Jeremiah 23). Shepherds must be trustworthy and willing to sacrifice for the well-being of their sheep (John 10).

In this metaphor there is a strong element of protection. The shepherd/pastor is called to be a watchperson to help safeguard the spiritual welfare of the people of God, both personal and communal. Pastors are to watch over the faithfulness of the people and help them guard against destructive elements intruding into their life and ministry.

2. The Pastor as One who Exercises Authority

The shepherd/pastor who watches over the people must know how to exercise authority, corresponding to the responsibility of the pastoral call. The exercise of spiritual authority in pastoral ministry is an expression of God's presence and God's reign.[6] This authority does not belong to the person of the pastor; it resides in the call by God and the church to the pastoral role; it is to be exercised under God with appropriate accountability to the church. Therefore, in the exercise of spiritual authority, the pastor does not "lord over" others (1 Peter 5:1-4), but serves as God's agent to call the people to live under the reign of God.

3. The Pastor as Minister of the Word

In Jeremiah, God lamented that there was no one to stand "in the council of the Lord, so as to see and to hear his word" and to give "heed to his word so as to proclaim it" (Jeremiah 23:18). Pastors are to be ministers of the Word, and through the Word call people to faithfulness in their relationship with God. For this, pastors must be well-trained in the use of Scripture. The church needs leaders who will discern the counsel of the Lord

---

[6]God's order, in which some are called to oversee the "flock," is essential to God's effective working in the world. The principle of oversight, in which one is called to assume some responsibility for another, is true not only for pastoral ministry but is also expressed in Scripture in terms of elder watching over younger and the stronger giving consideration to the weaker. This spiritual reality flies in the face of the concepts of autonomy, individualism, and self-realization so highly valued in our Western society. It is equally difficult for some who have an unbalanced view of the doctrine of the body of Christ or the priesthood of all believers in which it is held that since all are equal before God, all roles and positions must have equal authority in all things.

and help lead the community to prayerful listening, waiting, and hearing God. The discipline and faithfulness of the pastor's own encounter with the Word and with the counsel of the Lord is crucial for effective pastoral ministry in the life of the congregation.

4. The Pastor as Caregiver

The shepherd/pastor is to "strengthen the weak, heal the sick, bind up the injured, and bring back those who stray" (Ezekiel 34). Such people are often wounded or discouraged and need guidance and care. The pastor must attend to the spiritual well-being of person and community, wherever they are, and encourage them in their journey with God. This is the foundation of pastoral care.

Shepherding is a journey metaphor. Old Testament references view the shepherd as one who cares for the sheep so they can journey out, and each day return safely amid danger and need. Therefore, the practice of pastoral care must make the spiritual journey the primary concern. The ultimate focus of pastoral care must be the reign of God, not contemporary psychological understandings, important and helpful as they are.

The agenda of psychology to overcome internal and external conflicts, find inner peace, or pursue self-development is not identical to pastoral care; and it does not ultimately fulfill the agenda of pastoral care. True pastoral care has as its primary concern the care of the people so they can go on the journey and effectively fulfill the mission of the kingdom. Certainly God is interested in each detail of our life, and the pastor needs to help facilitate the search for inner peace and self-development; but these must be subject to the ultimate concern of the spiritual journey.

5. The Pastor as One Who is Trustworthy

In John 10 Jesus describes a shepherding relationship which requires both integrity and intimacy. The very nature of the role brings the shepherd/pastor into intimate relationship with people who are vulnerable. Jesus said the good shepherd comes in by the gate, not over the fence like thieves. This is an important word in a day when there are so many boundary violations among those in ministry.[7] It is essential that the shepherd/pastor

---

[7]Integrity is addressed in John 10:2. "The one who enters by the gate is the shepherd of the sheep." This is in contrast to the thief or bandit who climbs the fence – does not honor appropriate procedures and boundaries – for the purpose of personal gain. Intimacy is evident in John 10:3-4 where Jesus says of the good shepherd, "The sheep

have integrity and be trustworthy. He or she must not be devious in character, egocentric in nature, nor negligent in responsibility. He or she must help people avoid the pathways of destruction and point them to the way of life. And a trustworthy pastor is willing to sacrifice for the people rather than quickly run when there is danger or difficulty.

The shepherding metaphor, and the roles that so readily emerge from it, provides content to the meaning of incarnational presence. The shepherd expresses the nature of God's presence with the people of God. Even so, the concept of shepherd as a relevant metaphor for ministry today is likely to be difficult for the modern mind; it is drawn from a rural setting, and it may seem patriarchal. The shepherd/sheep analogy appears demeaning. However, the metaphor does reflect a very important reality for modern Christian experience. Jesus said, "The gate is wide and the road is easy that leads to destruction, and there are many who take it. For the gate is narrow and the road is hard that leads to life and there are few who find it" (Matthew 7:13-14). The Christian way is neither simple nor unambiguously clear. There are many dangers and deceptions along the way. God calls shepherds to help guide and support people on the way to life.

The spiritual oversight, responsibility, authority, and care that is inherent in the role of the shepherd need not be exercised in ways that are patriarchal or authoritarian. This metaphor does seem to reflect the reality that God calls persons in the body of Christ to a particular ministry in behalf of the whole. Shepherd/pastors are called to serve God by expressing God's care and guidance to the people. This call comes not because these persons (pastors) are more spiritual or more mature than others but because their particular ministry is essential to the reign of God.

D. The Minister as Helper (Advocate)

When Jesus announced that he was leaving, the disciples were disheartened and afraid. His presence seemed essential to their life and ministry. Nevertheless, in the Upper Room discourse (John 13-17), Jesus charges them with responsibility for continuing his work (14:12; 15:16; 17:18-19) and announces the advent of another presence (*paraklatos*). He promises that this presence will be alongside (*meta*) them as an advocate, among (*para*) them to create a new community in Christ, and within (*en*)

---

hear his voice. He calls his own sheep by name and leads them out..., he goes ahead of them, and the sheep follow him because they know his voice."

them to empower them for ministry (14:15-17). In this way the presence and ministry of the incarnate Jesus is to be multiplied in the world (14:12).

This presence is the Holy Spirit. Jesus identifies this Spirit as the Helper (*paraklatos*)[8] who is present to minister according to their need. When there is mourning, the Helper brings comfort. When one is in trouble, the Helper is an advocate. Jesus used this word to teach the disciples about the meaning of presence. The Helper will be with them forever (14:15), to remind them what Jesus taught (14:26), to witness to Jesus (15:26), to convict of sin (16:8), and to guide into all truth (16:13). In short, the Helper journeys with the people of God and provides what is needed for their life and mission. The Helper is present to comfort, counsel, teach, give wisdom, convict, heal, empower, encourage, and/or advocate, always according to the needs of each one and the community as a whole.

This concept of the Helper provides content and character to the nature of incarnational presence and helps define the function of ministry. This teaching is especially significant because it came at a time when Jesus was commissioning the disciples to carry on his ministry. It is a rich metaphor for ministry in that it links ministry to presence and provides some specifics for the function of ministry.

While it is true that the Helper is sent for all who minister in the name of Jesus, the pastor must be particularly attuned to this reality in order to be able to nurture understanding and receptivity of this presence in the people of God. The pastor incarnates this presence in the church by giving attention to the particular needs of the people in their journey and by teaching them to rely upon the Helper for their healing and hope.

Furthermore, it is essential in pastoral ministry to discern the movement of the Spirit and to join in with the purpose and work of the Helper. This enables the pastor to observe what God is doing and to minister more effectively in behalf of God and the Church. This also enables the pastor to help teach others to embrace and express this presence in their work and witness. In this way, the pastor joins the Helper in equipping and enabling the people of God in their mission.

---

[8]The Greek word *paraklatos* refers to a presence that may function in a variety of ways. Therefore, it is most often translated as either the Comforter, the Helper, or the Advocate. Helper seems to fit the versatile nature of this term as well as the intent of Jesus in reassurance of the disciples.

The concept of the helper can help inform our understanding of ministry. One way the presence of God continues in the world is through the Spirit/Helper who is in us, with us, and among us (14:15-17). This presence enables us in our own journey and empowers us for ministry with others. The helper models the nature of Christian ministry – to be present in the situation at hand, to be informed by human need and the desire of God, and to respond accordingly. This is a rich metaphor for understanding the ministry of pastoral care, pastoral counseling, and spiritual direction.

E. The Minister as Midwife

The use of this metaphor is relatively new in my own theological development, so I will only comment briefly on its usefulness for understanding ministry today. As I noted earlier, this metaphor informs me that God is the originator and sustainer of life. I as a minister am not the creator or bearer of life, but am called to attend to the spiritual birthing and growth process in others.

I believe this is a particularly important awareness in the ministry of presence. Like the midwife must trust and attend to the natural processes of birthing, so those who minister in the name of Christ must trust and attend to the spiritual birthing that is occurring whenever and wherever God is working. Those who engage in ministry must first of all see themselves as participants in a process that is beyond themselves. We as ministers do not initiate the process, we do not control the process, nor can we determine the outcome of the process. The midwife metaphor helps suggest how we are to be when called to the role of priest, shepherd, or helper. When clearly understood and accepted, this metaphor helps bring a spirit of *Gelassenheit*[9] to the work of ministry.

---

[9]*Gelassenheit* was an important concept in the life of the early Anabaptists. While difficult to translate simply in the English language, it denotes a radical trust and reliance upon God. One biblical example to illustrate this might be the story of the three Hebrews, Shadrach, Meshach, and Abednego (Daniel 3:24ff) whose radical faith led them to trust God in all circumstances. The midwife metaphor points to ministry as an active involvement with that which is already happening, the Spirit and power of God at work, along with a radical reliance upon God for the ultimate outcomes.

F. The Minister in the Body of Christ

The body of Christ as context helps determine the nature and function of ministry in the church. A sacramental ecclesiology is more concerned with the proper administration of the sacraments by a duly authorized person. A communal ecclesiology is concerned with the ministry of each one as well as the ministry of the pastoral office.

In Christian community, leaders are called to equip the body for ministry (Ephesians 4:11f). The goal of pastoral ministry in the congregation is to build up the body of Christ and to enable it to be a witness for God in the world. Pastoral ministry is to shepherd the church in its faithfulness to God.

Since there are many gifts in the body (1 Corinthians 12), there may be various persons who can help provide different elements of pastoral ministry. It is not likely that anyone can provide all the elements of pastoral ministry needed in the body. But it is clear that God calls certain persons and charges them with responsibility for shepherding the congregation. These persons are called not because they are more spiritual than others but because God chooses persons to do this work in God's behalf. Pastoral ministry is a unique calling in the church.

Perhaps as much as any of the metaphors considered in this study, the body of Christ is an expression of the continued presence of God in the world. First God came to be with us in the incarnation of Jesus. Then the Spirit was sent on the day of Pentecost to continue the presence of Christ. Now by the presence and empowerment of the Spirit, the church is an expression of the risen Christ in the world as those who have been baptized give witness to the presence and power of God among us. In this body some are called to pastoral ministry, a ministry of leadership: teaching, guiding, protecting, and warning, so the body may be faithful in the ministry of Christ.

IV. Conclusion

All ministry is rooted in the incarnation. Through the incarnation of Jesus, God has come to be with us, to have the true nature of the divine revealed to us, to identify with us in all circumstances, to call us to reconciliation and transformation. Like Abraham of old, God still calls people to partnership in mission; God still works through flesh and blood. As the presence of God is incarnate in the church, so the pastor is called to a particular embodiment of incarnation to help equip and enable the people of God to fulfill their mission in the reign of God. That is the foundation of ministry.

Priest, shepherd, helper, midwife, and body of Christ are metaphors that provide shape and substance to the concept of presence. These metaphors are expressions of God's presence and reflections of the character of God in our midst. They give meaning to the biblical declaration "God with us." They also help provide a theological rationale inherent in the role of the pastor.

The "office" of the pastor is a particular ministry of leadership, guidance, and enablement in the body of Christ. When the pastor functions appropriately as priest, shepherd, helper, and midwife, and helps lead the congregation in ministry that expresses the meaning of these metaphors, the incarnation is extended within and through the body of Christ into the world.

Chapter Ten

The Credibility of Leadership

George R. Brunk III

> This essay was originally given by George R. Brunk III as a presentation at Pastors' Week of Eastern Mennonite Seminary in January 1993. It was one of three presentations on ministry growing out of his interpretation of the Pastoral Epistles.

I. Introduction

In leadership, few things are as important as credibility. Credibility is the trait that makes authority effectual. Credibility is the quality that makes someone believable in the eyes of others. Only when a leader is "believed" will others respect the proffered leadership. Whatever may be the gifts of the leader and however prestigious the position, the people will respond to the exercise of leadership only if they consider the leader to be believable or, as we would more commonly say, trustworthy.[1] It is the idea of trust that best captures what is going on here.

Since a leader is one who by definition is out in front of the rest in one sense or another, the group needs to place trust in the leader for pointing the way that is not yet entirely clear and obvious to all. This role of trust or confidence is evident in all forms of leadership. It is given institutional form in the "vote of confidence" which is typical of democratic forms of social organization in society and church. Without the confidence of the group, a leader is ineffectual.

From where does credibility arise? What makes a leader credible or trustworthy? There is a clear answer offered to these questions by the Pastoral Epistles in the New Testament. These letters were written to a church leader and speak to issues of leadership in the church setting. The author has clearly reflected on the dynamics of successful and faithful leadership among the people of God. The trustworthy leader must give attention to two broad categories of life as the basis for his/her credibility. On the one side there needs to be a credible cause or message. On the other side is the need for a

---

[1] The reader should note that the words "credible," "believe," and "trust" all share the same root idea with the New Testament word for "believe – *pisteuo*."

credible character or personality. These stand out plainly in the following passage:

> These [the preceding faith affirmations] are the things you must insist on and teach. Let no one despise your youth, but set the believers an example in speech and conduct, in love, in faith, in purity (1 Timothy 4:11, 12).

The first area is represented in striking fashion by the "faithful sayings" which are a distinctive feature of the Pastorals. The author himself designates the sayings as "faithful." Now the word used here is precisely the Greek word for trustworthy or credible. It follows that credibility is here seen as pertaining to the vision of life that a leader embraces and promotes. The heart of this vision is, of course, the message of the gospel. Many of the faithful sayings state a fundamental truth of the gospel. However, some express a rather more secondary, even if important, truth for the welfare of the church's life. An illustration of the latter is the saying on which this study will focus. "The saying is sure: whoever aspires to the office of bishop [or overseer] desires a noble task" (1 Timothy 3:1).

The way in which the author expands on the saying just quoted illustrates very well the second aspect of the credibility of leadership, namely, the credible character and conduct of the leader. The well-known list of qualities for the bishop and deacon (1 Timothy 3:2-13), with its emphasis on the proven character of the leader, shows the implicit concern for credibility as the underlying point of view.

This brief overview of the Pastorals' perspective on church leadership points to an intricate interplay of dynamics in forming the credible leader. The presence of the "credible" sayings themselves in the letters is a statement of the fact that credibility in leadership involves something beyond the person of the leader. The Christian leader stands for the cause of God's kingdom. This is not only "the cause for which we stand." It is the cause by which one stands or falls as a leader. Faithful representation of this kingdom requires a true understanding of that kingdom. The faithful sayings form that right understanding and, consequently, create a sure place to stand for the leader. Credibility of the leader is an extension of the credibility of the vision for which he/she stands. If the message is believable, the messenger also has the opportunity to be believable as long as other factors do not contradict the fact.

But something new comes into view when the faithful sayings take up the subject of leadership itself as happens in 1 Timothy 3:1 and 4:7b-9. Now we read that not only do the great eternal verities of the gospel need to be credible to the church but the way leadership is viewed and the manner in which it is carried out must be the object of clear conviction. In other words, the credibility of leadership is dependent upon the understanding and persuasion that the believing community has about leadership in principle. For the church to be strong, it must believe that the role of leader among the people of God is indeed a noble task. It must be persuaded that training in godliness is the highest priority for the good church leader.

The picture is rounded out when we observe that the sayings concerning leadership have as their ultimate concern the selection and nurturing of leaders who possess the personal qualities of integrity upon which their credibility is also conditioned. This brings us back to the point of departure where it was observed that, in the Pastorals, leadership credibility consists in both the trustworthiness of the leader's program, i.e., the gospel, and of the leader's person.

This essay will look further at just one aspect of this larger picture. It is the question of how the church should look at the concept of leadership. This is the point made in the saying that "whoever aspires to the office of bishop desires a noble task."

II. Leadership is Noble

We must be careful not to misread the word "noble" in the saying. This translation could suggest a medieval social order marked by a sharp hierarchy. Such is far from the case. The word used by the author is the simple, common word for "good." Leadership is good! The English word "noble" here points to that which is of high and worthy value.

Care should also be taken not to understand the term "bishop" in an overly narrow sense. The term does not refer here to a leader of leaders. It appears to be the title of the main leader or leaders of the congregation who carry all leadership responsibilities not covered by the service ministry of the deacons. We are, therefore, justified in reading this faithful saying as a reference to the broad concept of leadership in the church.

This affirmation of the goodness of leadership is an indication that in the time of the early church, leadership did not enjoy high esteem and unqualified acceptance by everyone. Otherwise the point would not need to be made. It is not clear, however, where the problem may have lain. Perhaps in that context, the low view of leadership existed more among the leaders themselves rather than with those being lead. After all, the times placed particular demands on the leaders of a small and persecuted group.

But if the nobility of leadership was not self-evident in the early centuries, it is even more evident that twentieth-century Western society and church do not find it to be a credible claim. Leadership is not noble, and aspiration to it is at least questionable if not totally inappropriate. In our day, the problem exists first of all in the mind of the larger community. Only as a consequence of the fact that leadership is in low esteem at that level do the leaders themselves find it hard to see leadership as a good task. Small wonder that we have difficulty maintaining credible leadership. And the curious thing about all this is the fact that the church reflects pretty much the same attitude as the society in general.

The low view of leadership in our social context has many causes, no doubt. It is commonplace to describe our age as one that questions and restricts all authority – all authority, that is, except that of the individual and, perhaps, a small circle of like-minded persons. And this is only to trace the issue back to that other massive characteristic of our society, namely, individualism. The heritage of the Enlightenment with its justified reaction to arbitrary and uncritical authority has handed down to us a suspicion and subtle undermining of authority at all levels. Leadership, the necessary corollary of authority, is, at best, a necessary evil – not a good.

Yet another leading feature of our society that has also brought both weal and woe is egalitarianism – the equal significance and rights of every person. The effect of egalitarianism is the distribution of roles and functions that would otherwise tend to be concentrated in a few individuals. These individuals tend, in turn, to be the leaders of a given society or community. One could say that egalitarianism results in the diffusion of those social functions that constitute leadership. The problem that this has created is not the more democratic style of leadership that it brings, in which more persons share the roles of leading the larger community. The downside of this historical development has been the rise of an antileadership sentiment, as if egalitarian values inevitably exclude the relevance and importance of leadership.

The reality of leadership is still present in a strongly egalitarian social setting; it is merely distributed to a greater extent and may be less visible. But even in these cases, the community dare not presume to dispense with designated "leaders" who serve in coordinating and helping roles in order to make possible a healthy and productive community in which every individual is given the maximum opportunity to contribute to the common good and to influence group decisions.

The question of egalitarianism has taken on particular importance in some church settings and among Mennonites in particular. With their believers' church outlook, Mennonites have always emphasized the high status of the believer in the life of the church and have usually held a non-hierarchical view of leadership and authority. (Whether these ideals have always been observed or not is another matter.) The theological concept of the priesthood of all believers has been used, at least in recent times,[2] to undergird this perspective.

There has been a strong inclination in these recent decades to set the concept of priesthood of all believers over against the concept of designated leadership. The two ideals are then seen as mutually exclusive. The priesthood of all believers is understood to put each member on equal footing with the same level of privilege and responsibility but differing roles according to gift and calling. Designated leadership is seen as undermining these ideals by introducing inevitable differences of social level. What concept of leadership remains, if any, is of a role without structure that spontaneously moves from individual to individual in the exercise of a particular service to the community. The less visible it is, the better. In practice, the impression is gained that leadership is dispensable and unimportant. Leadership is certainly not noble.

What we must affirm is that leadership does indeed bring with it powerful temptations that threaten the biblical vision for community. The Christian virtues of humility and self-sacrificing love are ill at ease in the halls of leadership. But such problems do not prove that leadership is inherently evil. To the contrary! The fact that it is so vulnerable to abuse is indirect evidence of its essential place in human experience. The higher the moral value of a thing, the greater its potential for distortion. The issue for the church is not whether leadership is good. The only question is what kind of leadership is good.

Does empirical observation confirm the credibility of the Pastorals' saying? Does historical experience verify it? I am convinced that they do. First, it is simply a fact of life that groups cannot function well and be

---

[2]Recent research has questioned whether the priesthood of all believers was used by the sixteenth-century Anabaptists in the sense we are talking about it here. See the article in *The Mennonite Encyclopedia, Vol. V.*, "Priesthood of All Believers."

enduring if there is an absence of identifiable leadership. It is an observable fact that groups do not and cannot operate without the assisting role of one or more individuals who are recognized and empowered by the members of the group to carry out certain special tasks that make it possible for the group to work together. As a pure collectivity, a group cannot function. It can only do so when an individual, on behalf of the group, takes certain initiatives such as calling the group together, helping it make decisions, providing the resource of ideas and vision, and the like. (This is, in fact, a possible definition of leadership.) Moreover, even though any member might spontaneously fill one of these leadership roles, a group cannot depend solely on such initiatives on the part of individuals.

Chaos is engendered when a group waits on private initiative alone. At some level there must be persons who are recognized by the entire group as carrying standing responsibilities. Where there is no predictability, based on mutual agreement, about how a group will proceed in its common life, frustration and fragmentation follow. Designated leadership is a key part of that predictability. In the vision of the New Testament, the ideal pattern of leadership involves a designated leadership that creates the orderly context within which the "charismatic"[3] or spontaneous form of leadership by all members can operate. These two forms of leadership can easily compete with one another for control. The dominant tendency is for the designated leadership to suppress the "charismatic" in response to this threat. Such leadership is referred to as authoritarian.

These observations find confirmation in the history of the people of God from biblical times to the present. The clear and overwhelming impression one takes from this history is that good times for the people of God are always times of conspicuous and strong leadership. These may be times of key turns in the form of God's purpose for the world and for his people. Noah, Abraham, Moses, and Jesus are leader figures at such times. The periods of renewal and mission advance are also such times.

---

[3]The word "charismatic" is used here in its technical sense, meaning a type of leadership that is based purely on the ability of the individual to carry out a leadership role outside of traditional organizational structures and offices. The emphasis on ability or gift relates the idea to the New Testament teaching on spiritual gifts given to all believers. All good leadership must be based on gift. The point we are making is that certain roles of leadership must, in addition to gift, be characterized by formal, public designation.

The Martin Luthers, the Menno Simons, the John Wesleys, and the William Careys are examples. From this we can also conclude that in all times and places, there is a relationship between leadership and the health of the church. This is not to say that strong leadership is enough to guarantee a strong church. Not all "strong" leadership is necessarily good leadership and factors other than leadership are determinative for the spiritual well-being of God's people. Nevertheless, there has been no time in history, biblical or otherwise, when God's people flourished and leadership languished.

This last observation about the experience of history demonstrates that strong community is not in antithesis to strong leadership. In fact, the two complement one another. It is the same complementarity that exists between community and individual. On first thought, these two words stand in contrast and conflict. And at times they do. However, in the normal and ideal experiences of life, community and individual depend on each other and reinforce one another. The community lives from the initiatives and gifts of individuals who compose it; the individual lives from the support of the community which forms him/her. The two draw their strength from each other. Both can be strong if each is committed to the good of the other. The same dynamic exists between community and leader.

In a certain sense, we can say that leadership is inevitable. One can easily observe that where legitimate (community approved) leadership is despised and downplayed, some type of illegitimate leadership quickly appears. Since what appears is unrecognized, it tends to go unnoticed and persons convince themselves that they have put leadership "in its place." But strong personalities emerge and determine the direction of the group. A kind of shadow leadership arises. One can only conclude that groups do not reject leadership. They only reject particular forms of leadership and leaders. The parallel to this is that we do not rebel against authority, for authority too is inevitable for humans and human community. We rebel against a particular expression of authority.

The saying is indeed sure and believable – "Whoever aspires to [lead God's people] desires a noble (good) task."

III. Leadership is Desirable

The presence of the two words "aspire" and "desire" in our faithful saying are as difficult for some readers as the idea that leadership of God's people is good. This reaction even finds some ground in the fact that the word used here for "desire" is the word used to describe the impulses of human nature that attract us into sin. A positive meaning for the word is rare in the New Testament. However, we may find some clue for right understanding in noting that, for biblical writers, the desires of the body are good gifts of God. But where enmity with God exists, these desires drive us to realize selfish and evil ends rather than good ends. Evil uses what is good in itself as an instrument for achieving evil. To have desires is not wrong. The question always is: "To what end does a particular desire aspire?"

The observation has been made that the best leaders are those who do not aspire to the position. The reluctant leader, who accepts the request of a group, is the one who better represents the interests of the community rather than his/her own interests. Such a leader has the self-image of a servant. Ambition tends to cloud the vision of what leadership actions are most needed for the corporate good. There is profound truth in this line of thought, and it seems to undermine the credibility of the "faithful saying."

Moreover, in much of the Mennonite tradition, with its strong emphasis on the virtue of humility, the idea of aspiring to a position of prominence and power has been frowned upon. Even where a call to public ministry was felt, the individual did not make this known nor take initiatives to help bring it to realization. The church had to take all action in the implementation. Here any form of ambition appears to be excluded because it totally contradicts the definition of Christian virtue.

How shall we respond to this picture? From the point of view of the faithful saying, there is a connection between the goodness of leadership and the appropriateness of aspiration to be a leader. If something is good, it ought to be desirable for the righteous person. Furthermore, and more likely to evoke dispute, if something is not perceived to be desirable in some sense, it will not be considered good.

Christians often hold the view that the values of self-denial, love of neighbor, humility, and the like, exclude all self-interest and personal aspiration. The biblical writings reflect another perspective. By teaching a positive view of reward and of self (love your neighbor as yourself) they imply that there is a form and degree of self-interest that is compatible with the altruistic vision of biblical faith. It is the nature of the case that true fulfillment for the community is not possible apart from fulfillment for the individuals who make up the community. (The opposite is also true.) True, we sometimes must deny personal interests in order to achieve corporate interests. But this is in the short term. In the longer term, the interests of the community and the individual must be parallel. If not, we would dehumanize the person contrary to the creation purposes of God. In Christian eschatology, for example, the ultimate fulfillment of the community and the individual is the same.

The church has been inclined to what we could call an ascetic view of leadership – a self-sacrificing hardship that some members of the church must undertake in order to achieve a spiritual goal. This one-sided view, applied to the total Christian life, was already present in the early church. The Pastorals had to struggle against it as 1 Timothy 4:3 expressly says. In contrast to an ascetic view, "everything created by God is good, and nothing to be rejected, provided it is received with thanksgiving. . ." (1 Timothy 4:4). "Provided. . . !" This is the operative word. Everything is good and worthy of being desired, on condition that its end is not in the created thing itself or for the sole interest of the human person. So we can say that to aspire to a position of leader is a legitimate self-interest, provided that the self-interest is compatible with and complementary to the interests of God and of God's people. That, of course, is a tall order and susceptible to distortion by our self-centeredness. But the attempt to suppress the self entirely only exposes us to another set of distortions and temptations.

The failure to be able to affirm a "holy ambition" to leadership exacts a heavy toll on the life of the church. While this stance, no doubt, discourages the persons who might want to take advantage of the church out of selfish motives, it also discourages the sincere and well-meaning person who sees the rewards as inadequate and who resists the call to sacrifice from a church that, out of its own selfishness, adds unnecessary sacrifice to the necessary. Recent lack of candidates for the pastoral roles in Mennonite congregations has rightly been traced, at least in part, to these factors.[4]

The reluctance to affirm a sanctified aspiration to church leadership causes another problem as well. The subtle invitation not to acknowledge one's sense of call to this role lest one fall into the sin of ambition, places these persons in a position where the call cannot be cultivated and reinforced by the community. As a result, these individuals must pursue other vocations, including educational preparation, until the church issues a call. One can only wonder how many there are whom God has called but who have suppressed the call, perhaps to the point of oblivion.

---

[4] This is a reference to the Pastorate Project carried out by the two largest Mennonite bodies in North America and administered by the Mennonite Board of Education (Mennonite Church).

These comments are not intended to reduce the significance of discernment and calling by the church. Here again, as we have seen at various points, the individual and the community ought not be set against one another. The individual should be encouraged to make public the inner stirrings of the Spirit from childhood on; the church should engage the individual in weighing the call's validity and in defining its exact vocational expression.

IV. Conclusion

Yes, we can and must embrace as faithful the saying "Whoever aspires to the office of [church leader] desires a noble task." This is a credible place for the church to take its stand with regard to leadership. Leadership is a good and noble thing, and to aspire to it is altogether acceptable. If we are to experience good leadership in the church, we must begin with this belief and act on it. The credibility of our leaders begins with the credence of the church in leadership. Not that the credibility of a leader ends there. That is the beginning point, but only that. Credibility, as the Pastorals show, involves other areas just as crucial to successful leadership. The leader must hold and articulate a credible message about the things of God. And the leader must exemplify in credible conduct the reality of the message. This particular faithful saying may not constitute an article of faith on which the church either stands or falls. But issues of leadership shake the foundations of the church and destabilize its life about as quickly as anything. Therefore, the church needs some firm place to stand in these matters. This faithful saying is a good place to begin.